Even as the alchemist builds on the discoveries of his predecessors, so there is an inner teacher within every heart who tutors the outer self, subduing it when necessary and guiding the fires of the mind in their search for the oftentimes invisible strands of reality.

Saint Germain

Intermediate
Studies in
Alchemy

Alchemical Formulas for
Self-Mastery

Saint Germain

Dictated to the Messenger
Mark L. Prophet

Summit University Press®
Los Angeles

Intermediate Studies in Alchemy
Published by
SUMMIT UNIVERSITY PRESS

LIBRARY OF CONGRESS CATALOG CARD NUMBER: 74-82295
INTERNATIONAL STANDARD BOOK NUMBER: 0-916766-01-2

This book is set in 10.5 News with 2 points of lead

Printed in the United States of America

Fourth Printing

Summit University Press®
Los Angeles

Table of Contents

Wherein lies happiness? In that which becks
Our ready minds to fellowship divine,
A fellowship with essence; till we shine,
Full alchemiz'd, and free of space. Behold
The clear religion of heaven!

Keats, *Endymion*

Foreword

Change is the order of the day. Change is the means whereby we make the transition from the old order to the new, from the human to the divine. Change is the catalyst for the increased awareness of the potential of man. Change is necessary for the very survival of a planet and a people.

Alchemy is the science of change. *Intermediate Studies in Alchemy* written by Saint Germain is a sequel to his initial work, *Studies in Alchemy*. Both volumes were originally a series of letters dictated by the master Saint Germain to his students throughout the world. Set forth by the messenger Mark L. Prophet, they were published by The Summit Lighthouse as *Pearls of Wisdom*.

Saint Germain is the master alchemist. Through the scientific application of the principles of change, this ascended master, who once walked the earth an alchemist of both Matter and Spirit, won his freedom from the wheel of rebirth and stands today a perfected one. He imparts to his readers basic and advanced techniques from the all-chemistry of God with the supreme goal of providing them with the formula for transcending the former self and becoming the Christed self.

The purpose of the master's writing is to communicate a spiritual yet altogether scientific means of raising consciousness to receive the vibrations of the new age. To Saint Germain, the hierarch of the Aquarian age, man is not truly free until he has the power to create. He teaches that to be free to create, man must channel the stream of energy that God is giving to him in ceaseless descent into matrices of creative desire patterned after the divine will; but when he misqualifies these energies, they form the links of the chain that binds him.

The work of the alchemist is the work of God in man. It is not man subjecting the energies of God to the confinements of his human will, but it is God in man liberating man's energies to the fulfillment of the creative mandate "Take dominion over the earth." Following step by step Saint Germain's instruction, the alchemist comes into the awareness of his true self as God and of himself as the Great Alchemist in physical form. Centered in the flaming Presence of the I AM THAT I AM, man the alchemist puts on the consciousness of God the Alchemist and thereby discovers the key to obey the divine injunction "Create!"

Alchemy is the gift of God to man whereby he can find forgiveness of sin, the changing of the waters of the human consciousness into the wine of the Spirit, and the restoration of the essential sacredness of life that has been lost. Alchemy is the science that Saint Germain demonstrates to unlock the miracles of the Christ and to make them available to all who believe in the omnipresent Spirit. Alchemy is the means whereby man receives the gift of the kingdom which is the Father's good pleasure to give to all.

ELIZABETH CLARE PROPHET
Messenger for
the Great White Brotherhood

Retreat of the Resurrection Spiral
Colorado Springs, Colorado

I

"Create!"

To All Alchemists and Would-be Alchemists, Salutations!

When the Great Alchemist's Spirit breathed into man's nostrils the breath of life, the fire of creative Spirit filled the clay tabernacle. An embryonic god was born.

The practical aspects of alchemy are to be found in manifestation only in the one who has developed the power to execute the design of freedom. Whatsoever bindeth is not the friend of the alchemist; yet it is the goal of the alchemist to bind the soul to its immortal tryst in order that the pact of life might be sanctified even as the precious gift of individual identity is accepted.

Now the identity of the alchemist is to be found in the mandate "Create!" And in order that he might obey, the fiery energies of creation are dispensed to him each moment. Like crystal beads descending upon a crystal thread, the energies of the creative essence of life descend into the chalice of consciousness. Neither halting nor delaying in their appointed course, they continue to fall into the

repository of man's being. Here they create a
buildup for good or for ill as each iota of universal
energy passes through the recording nexus and is
imprinted with the fiat of creation.

The fiat reflects the intent of the will of the
individual monad. When the fiat is withheld, there
is an idling of the great cosmic furnace as the talent
of the descending chaliced moment is rejected by
the consciousness and becomes an opportunity lost.
Where there is no qualification, no fiat of intent, the
energy retains only the God-identification of the
talent without the stamp of individualization; and
thus it falls into the coffers of the lifestream's
record without having received so much as an erg
of qualification.

The creative process, then, is of little signif-
icance to the individual who does not recognize
the mandate to create, for by his nonrecognition
he forfeits his God-given prerogative. As a result
of man's neglect of his responsibility, the fiat of
God was given that is recorded in the Book of
Revelation: "Thou art neither cold nor hot: I
would thou wert cold or hot. So then because thou
art lukewarm, and neither cold nor hot, I will spue
thee out of my mouth."[1]

The fiat to create must be heeded, but let us
pray God that men heed well the sovereign
responsibility that Life has given them to create
after the pattern of the divine seed. Well might they
emulate the elder gods of the race and the royal
priesthood of the order of Melchizedek in their
creative endeavors, that they might convey upon
the energy chain of life that peculiar and fasci-
nating aspect of cosmic genius that is the nature
of the eternal God.

So long as individuals allow themselves to be
kept in a state of constant fear, so long as they deny

themselves the great benefits of universal hope, so long as they fail to take into account the meaning of the promise "His mercy endureth for ever,"[2] so long shall they continue in ignorance to deny themselves the bliss that exudes from the rightful exercise of spiritual privilege.

To belittle the soul of man, to cast it down into a sense of sin, frustration, and self-condemnation is the work of the princes of darkness. But it is ever the forte of the sons of heaven, of the ascended masters, and of the cosmic beings to elevate that supreme nobility which is both the fabric and the content of the soul into such prominence in the life of man that he might hear the dominant word of the eternal God in ringing tones, "Thou art my Son; this day have I begotten thee."[3]

Man must enter into a pact of universal trust based on his own inner commitment to the grace of God that will not prohibit him from exercising the power of the living Word to emulate the masters, to emulate the Only Begotten of the Father, to emulate the Spirit of comfort and truth. And when he does, he will find opening to his consciousness a new method of cleansing his soul by the power of the Lord's Spirit. Then he will come to understand the meaning of the statement made concerning Abraham of old that Abraham's faith "was imputed unto him for righteousness: and he was called the Friend of God."[4]

And so it is "not by might, nor by power, but by my Spirit, saith the Lord of hosts"[5] that man accomplishes the alchemical feat of transmuting the base metals of human consciousness into the gold of Christed illumination. Human might and human power can never change man's darkness into light, nor can they deliver humanity from the sense of struggle that bans from their lives the acknowledgment of the God-given potential that lies within the domain of the self.

The victorious accomplishments of the Master Jesus, together with the "greater works" which he promised that the disciples of Christ would do "because I go unto my Father,"[6] remain in this age, as in ages past, a fiat of universal freedom. Thus the works of the alchemists of the Spirit beckon the souls of men to forsake their attitudes of self-condemnation, self-pity, self-denegation, self-indulgence, and overreaction to the errors of the past. For when men learn to forgive and forget their own mistakes, their hearts will rejoice in the acceptance of the word from on high "What God hath cleansed, that call not thou common."[7]

Recognizing, then, that the potential of every man rests in his immersion in the great soundless-sound stream of living light-energy from the heart of the universal Christ, we say: Let the power of the Holy Spirit, worlds without end, exert its mighty cosmic pressures upon the soul of the would-be alchemist until he emerges from the fiery furnace pliable, whited, and pure in the willingness to obey the fiat of the Lord to create first a clean heart and then to renew in self a right spirit.

God is a Spirit; and as the Supreme Alchemist who has the power to work change in the universe, he is able to convey his passion for freedom to the soul of any man who will accept it. His is the passion which produces in man the miracle of unfoldment through a sense of the real. His is the passion that will drive from the temple those money changers and bargainers who would literally sell the souls of men in the marketplaces of the world.

We are concerned with creating in the student of alchemy a conscious awareness of the power of the Spirit to convey the transmutative effect of the Universal Alchemist into the lives and beings of embodied humanity. It is through this awareness that they shall be exalted in a manner which they have never before experienced, for at last they shall have recognized that within themselves the cosmic key-seed of universal potential lies literally entombed.

To resurrect then the Spirit of the Cosmic Alchemist means that we must seek before we shall find, that we must knock before the door shall be opened. We must, in the ritual of true faith, be content to commit ourselves to him who is able to keep and to save to the uttermost those who believe in his manifold purposes. These are centralized in the one purpose of unfolding the consciousness of the stone which the builders have rejected,[8] of the Christ that is the head of every man.

In the concept of the abundant life is to be found the radioactive principle of the expanding God consciousness into which any man may drink without depriving his brother of one iota of his inheritance. There is no need then for jealousy or a sense of struggle to function in the lives of the true alchemists; and wise are they who will submit themselves to the pressures of the divine law, who will seek to purge themselves of all unclean habits stemming from mortal density and of doubt and fear, which are the root cause of man's nonfulfillment of his destiny.

Those who dare to submit to the will of God will come to the place where their souls can at last welcome, face to face, the overcoming Spirit that makes possible the transfer of the consciousness of the Great Alchemist to the consciousness of the lesser alchemist. Through this transfer, hope is amplified in the microcosm of self and the miracle of emerging chrysalis is beheld. Then the soul, feeding upon the living Word which throbs within, finally understands its raison d'être in the fiat of the light "Create!"

It is incumbent upon each life, then, to create according to the patterns made in the heavens.[9] He who can produce the miracle of these patterns in his life is also able to have all things added unto him; for by his seeking first the kingdom of heaven, the earth herself yields to his dominion.

In this series on intermediate alchemy, I am, in the name of Almighty God, creating in the consciousness of the disciples who apply themselves to this study a spirit of inner communion. Through this spirit—a focus of my own flame— the Most High God and the hierarchy of light shall focus, by the power of universal Love, a climate within the consciousness of the student that shall enable him to obtain his rightful place in the divine scheme. Then the kingdom will flower and men will perceive that they need not engage in struggle or seek by violent means to obtain that which God is ever ready to give unto them.

The lingering fear in the worlds of men is of the dark, whereas faith, hope, and charity are the great triune bearers of light who exalt reality and lead men toward the light.

Ready for action,

I remain the Knight Commander,

II

Practical Alchemy

To Those Who Are Willing to Follow
  in His Footsteps:

The history of man's devotion to the cause of
freedom may never be written either for the planet
or for the individual; therefore, man will never
know by outward study the true story of freedom.
Nevertheless, through the outreach of the Spirit of
God in man and its wondrous attunement with the
central clearing house for every part of life, he may
enter into the akashic records of those solemn
moments in the lives of other men and thereby
perceive how they obtained their victory.

Even as the alchemist builds on the discoveries of his predecessors, so there is an inner
teacher within every heart who tutors the outer
self, subduing it when necessary and guiding the
fires of the mind in their search for the oftentimes
invisible strands of reality.

When the subject of creation is given more
than ordinary consideration, man begins to realize
that his own destiny lies as a gift in his hands. He
has always looked to God for assistance, and God

has always looked to man that he might convey
to him every good gift and all the support which
man could reasonably receive and acknowledge.
Unfortunately, even in those periods of their most
advanced meditations, mankind have seldom
glimpsed the necessary cosmic pattern of what
they are and what they shall be.

The secrets of alchemy are always to be found
in the domain of creation. If man has not the power
to create, he is not truly free. Therefore, the stream
of energy that God is giving to him in ceaseless
descent must needs be channeled into matrices of
creative desire patterned after the divine will; but
when misqualified, these energies form the links of
the chain that binds him.

Our first step, then, is to abort and to
transmute the negatively qualified substance in the
world of every would-be alchemist. The power of
the violet transmuting flame, as an agent of the
Holy Spirit, can be called forth from God for the
purification of man's world. It should be noted,
however, that this power is seldom recognized until
the alchemist has invoked the flame for a
considerable period of time. But, practice as he
will, his use of the flame will not be enough to
transform his world unless the correct scientific
attitude is maintained. The alchemist who insists
on exalting his own human will and ego in
contradistinction to the Divine Will and Ego cannot
possibly receive the great gifts which the Spirit
seeks to convey.

I know that many people are reluctant to
release themselves completely into the hands of
God. They are willing to go part of the way, and
they gingerly step forward when the higher will
seems to flatter their own; but because they have
not let go of the human will, they find in the end that

their efforts are unrewarded. Man cannot bargain with God. Nevertheless, Cosmos is far more ready to give every good and perfect gift to man than man is ready to receive it. The problem, then, lies not in the ocean that is filled with pearls, but in the diver himself, who must be willing to acknowledge the presence of the treasures of heaven in the cosmic depths—treasures that Heaven intends man not only to discover but also to possess.

By incorrect attitudes, men have kept themselves from the kingdom of heaven. They have sought through magic and, unfortunately, even through witchcraft to win for themselves that which could be obtained on a permanent basis only by willing submission to the will of God, to his intents and his purposes.

How long will men deceive themselves? How long will they prevent themselves, by their fears, from surrendering to the living purposes of God? It is as though they would not relinquish their money to the merchants in the shops until they held in hand the intended purchase. There is no bargaining with God or with Cosmos. Cosmos is ever willing to convey the highest and best gifts to man; but in order to receive them, man must change his attitude.

Those who are schooled in the knowledge of the world may believe in their hearts that they have found through academic pursuits the key to the governing of the senses and to gaining entrée into the realms of the Spirit. We say, not so! For neither by intellect nor by self-righteousness shall men obtain the highest gifts. These gifts will come as the natural unfoldment of the soul who submits to the grace of God and understands that having done so, he can rightfully expect the divine revelation to manifest within himself. And when that revelation comes forth, it is received within the hallowed circle of righteousness and reason—a righteousness that does not do despite to his neighbor, that seeks no harm to any, and a reason that understands that the best gifts of the Spirit relate to the realm of the practical.

The practicality of God must not be employed as a weapon to destroy the mystical beauties of the Spirit. On the contrary, it must be used to draw the divine mystery to the focal point of individual manifestation. As the flesh came forth and was animated by the Spirit, so practicality must come forth and be animated by the creative purposes of God. Then God will take man by the hand and lead him through the realm of perfect order to a place where man will perceive that the world and all things in it were originally created according to a perfect cosmic pattern. Here he will be shown that each individual was intended to manifest a specific facet of the divine intent and that each facet of the grand design was created to complement the other and to produce thereby the miracle beauty of an everlasting kingdom, worlds without end.

How can men imagine that the Mind that created man in all of his wondrous parts—the universe, the stars, the suns, the spiritual realms— would be so lacking in foresight as to fail to provide a way of escape for those who might wander from the cosmic blueprint? Did not his practicality bestow upon man the fullness of the divine conveyance expressed in the command "Take dominion over the earth"?[1] Man, then, was and is intended to be a practical manifestation of God, learning how to master his environment by cosmic wisdom united with his own natural intelligence.

We have seen, however, that man becomes

discouraged when he realizes that although he has exercised his mental faculties to the point where his mind is literally crammed with an encyclopedic knowledge of the world, he is nevertheless mentally muscle-bound and powerless to take dominion over his personal affairs—much less the earth—because he is spiritually anemic.

Now such discouragement is the result of the individual's failure to recognize the fact that he is actually a monadic part of God. He does not know— for he has not been told—that in his silent eternal union with the mind of God, he is tied to a giant computer. Through this computer all knowledge is immediately available by spiritual transmission to those who will use it to do the will of God. But the bounds of man's habitation—including the bounds of his mental probings—which are prescribed by cosmic law, cause this wisdom to be withheld from that part of the universe which is not yet ready to assume its role in taking dominion over the earth and in making itself functional with the powers of the universal Christ.

The key, then, to the practice of advanced spiritual alchemy lies in the alchemist's understanding of the purposes of the Brotherhood and in his consciously yoking himself together with those who are pledged by word and deed to the fulfillment of those purposes. Little do men realize when they begin to pursue the study of alchemy how deeply involved it will become and how deeply they will become involved in it. For unless there is an immersion of the self in the sea of universal wisdom and purpose, the soul cannot be saturated, the sponge cannot be wetted, and the energy so needed for transmutation cannot be evoked.

If I seem to be releasing the secrets of the

ages slowly into the minds of the hurried and harried students who would like to overcome all things in a moment, let me say that you today are receiving from the retreats of the Brotherhood more information than we ourselves received in the past when we were undertaking our own novitiate. In your patience, then, possess ye your souls;[2] but be diligent in studying the various aspects of being which from time to time will be pointed out to you— sometimes from the most unexpected sources. Be ready to find in the smallest gift an intricate treasure that, like a piece in a great puzzle, may not at first seem relevant.

Again I say, be patient. For time, in marching on, reveals eternal patterns. Therefore, to decline the search or to reject the means of cosmic study which makes possible the search is an error of the first magnitude. Let all who are receiving this form of instruction rejoice and be glad, seeing in the very opportunity for self-study the need to render the service to the brothers of acquainting others with the teaching. Thus by making available the gift of life to receptive souls, Heaven shall respond and give a greater gift to the souls of you who have proven that you are willing to labor and to wait.

Perfection is forthcoming; and it is the perfection of a master mason—a builder who, in idealizing perfection in the universe, has no alternative but to idealize it in himself. This is the builder who sees the need to cleanse the very foundation of residue in his world, to submit to the washing of the water by the Word[3] and to the cleansing of the sacred fire. This is the builder who sees the need to know what the tools of the aspirant are and how these tools may be employed in the service of self, in the service of humanity, and thus ultimately in the service of his God.

Let us then reiterate for all
That life is not so simple as men have dreamed.
But it is a scheme so vast and tall
As to literally enfold us all—
Men and gods and masters, too,
Parts of life you do not view
Right now, but one day will
If you will only learn to listen and be still,
Knowing I AM God within.

To his glory I live,

Saint Germain

III

Spiritual Alliance

To All Who Would Aid the Cause
   of Mankind's Victory:
   Little does the beginning alchemist realize the
need for a spiritual alliance. If men are critical of
the appearance of oppositional aspects in religious
endeavor such as struggles among the brethren,
their ungodly attitudes, their criticism, condemnation, and judgment of one another, let them
realize that that which is below is not the product
of that which is above, but remains a part of human
creation which is no real part of God.
   It is to genuine spiritual brotherhood, then,
that we would direct your attention, for the alchemist who seeks but his own unfoldment can never
manifest aught but a relatively weak potential.
Those who ally themselves with the Brotherhood of
light are utilizing the functional power of the Great
Alchemist not as a mighty ocean pouring through a
narrow inlet, but as the great ocean roaring to the
perfection of itself. Thus in all true striving, the
hand, aware of the head, blesses the feet that
march in progress toward an appointed goal.

Freedom then is a name and a game, but the stakes are very high. The Great Alchemist demands absolute obedience from every adherent and from all who would practice the game of victorious becoming.

Man is a limited creature. He is limited by the mésalliances he has formed, often in the bane of ignorance. Therefore, we must commence by literally turning the being of man upside down and inside out. We must ferret out the little tricks that have been employed by the finite self in maintaining its own sovereignty over the lives of others, for it is the sense of struggle that has actually created a struggle in the lives of countless millions. But when they shed that sense, when they perceive that the universe is a harmonious working-together of light serving light, they will hasten to be about the Father's business of transmuting the shroud that covers the earth, the shroud that is composed of the elements of mankind's own insanity and destructive emotional patterns.

The sacred fire has been distorted through the misuse of sex, and sacred music has been aborted through the introduction of astral and voodoo rhythms. The new moralities of the people must be seen for what they are—simply the old and sordid outworkings of Sodom and Gomorrah come again. Children are taught to pay homage to personalities, and thus they follow after rock'n'roll idols who themselves are the victims of the demons of darkness. The brutal noises of these pied pipers jar the fine sensibilities of the soul and destroy the inner electronic machinery that would enable the youth to attune with the Spirit of God and to decipher the tongues of angels.

The game now is to draw the youth into a spirit

of rebellion before they have the opportunity of developing a correct understanding of life and of their destiny[1] as heirs of God. But I cannot honestly say that their elders have excelled in virtue, nor do I find that the power of example has been spread abroad in the world as it should. The ancient proverb "Train up a child in the way he should go: and when he is old, he will not depart from it"[2] has failed of expression in many generations. Nevertheless, we must not destroy the foundation of hope in the world; for although there have been failures, there have also been numerous successes, many of them unchronicled in the annals of the race.

And so whereas we do indeed, and rightly so, condemn mankind's increasing lack of morality, their licentious spirit and struggle for ego-expression, and whereas we do condemn the violent and indiscriminate overthrow of institutions and standards long upheld by the Brotherhood as guidelines for the working out of karmic imbalances, we also accede that an enormous amount of God's energy has been misqualified in this and past ages. Therefore, the trends toward misqualification must be challenged at the same time that they are being reckoned with as karmic factors by those who are determined to override man's density and to bring into manifestation the long-awaited kingdom.

Have men failed in the past? Then the record of that failure is a magnet to draw them down, and strong counteracting forces must be kindled. The power of heaven must be reharnessed and men must turn from darkness toward the light. There is, then, a purpose for spiritual alchemy. But before I go into it enough to enable you to draw forth greater measures of cosmic energy and to learn how to qualify this energy correctly, I must show the relevance of this study to the present age.

The destructive energies which poured through the Beatles and entered the subconscious minds of the youth, popular though they were in the world of form, are gradually working their way to the surface, revealing their true colors and satanic origins. These unholy emanations have drawn many young souls into the mistaken belief that the taking of drugs, the practice of witchcraft, and illicit sex can give them freedom from all imposed limitations. Instead, these indulgences have held them in bondage to the legions of darkness.

Would it not be then of greater value and virtue if the resurgent power of regeneration were allowed to come forth through many hearts as a great cosmic flow? The forward movement of this flow is able to engender in men a spirit of willing acceptance of cosmic beauty, which in turn brings about the flowering of hope in the youth—hope for a greater measure of inward satisfaction, hope for a greater measure of attunement with the realities of the universe. For the tides of reality continually pour through the cosmos whether man is aware of them or not.

The certitudes of life are often unknown by the young in heart who, while they are borne upon the tide of human events, are seldom able to compass those events with a relevancy that would give greater meaning to their lives. I am therefore advising all to eschew the evil and darkness that enter the forcefield of the four lower bodies when the attention is placed on the jangle of modern jazz. I advise all who would truly be alchemists of the Spirit to seek out the classical music of the world's greatest composers—of Beethoven, Bach, Chopin, Haydn, Handel, Wagner, Liszt, Mozart,

Mendelssohn, Mahler, and many others who have been commissioned by the Brotherhood to bring forth the music of the spheres.

I advise all to learn to seek in meditation those peaks of cosmic elevation that will enable them to understand and interpret the language of the angels. I advise all to take the time to learn what is real and to develop passions of genuine love toward humanity. But let not these passions take the form of mere devotion to communal efforts or to the raising of one segment of life into a more advanced state of economic development; rather let them take the form of raising men to new levels of spiritual appreciation of their own divine potential as sons of God.

Only by this form of devotion shall their hearts, touched by the hands of the Infinite Creator, be imbued with such reality and love that they will move with precision to execute the divine will. Thus shall men behold the outworkings of a Providence that has for so long yearned to find greater expression in mortal affairs, that those affairs might become truly guided by the power of Life from on high.

Then shall liberty live in human lives. Then shall freedom in honor raise men to a state where they can invoke, by the creative power of the Spirit, a golden age that will transcend the age of Pericles and every other golden age that the earth has ever known. This shall come about through the establishment of a fountain of living flame-power, -wisdom, and -love.[3]

That fountain shall inundate the souls of men and drench their garments with so much of the essence of freedom that they will perceive spiritual alchemy as the means to every cosmic end. And the glory of the threefold flame, now saturating their consciousness with a fiery brilliance, will evoke an equal response in the very heart of God. The bond thus established between earth and heaven shall raise this star to a position of greater brilliance than the Star of the East that heralded the approach of the Master Jesus two thousand years ago, for this light will signify the victory of the Christ consciousness not only in one Son of God, but also in all mankind.

I am the exponent of freedom for this age; and in revealing these facts about the science of alchemy, I cannot restrain myself from voicing these sentiments as apropos of the struggles of the times. Are men filled with idealism? Let them turn that idealism toward the light where divine ideas flow out from a central fountain of living flame. There let all kindle and rekindle the torches of being, and let the fires of their minds be saturated with new hope for a new age born of the Spirit.

Life was never meant to be a cesspool of defeat, but a pillar of victory whose crowning laurel speaks of a living abundance. Blooming within the soul, that abundance extends itself out of the lonely room of self into the larger domain of the universe. The ascended masters' consciousness is a vital power which will assist the devotee in performing a more than ordinary activity of genuine service and renewal. For we are about the Father's business of renewing the consciousness of men—not by applying old patches over old patches, but by renovating the entire garment of consciousness.

As we prepare then to make the would-be spiritual alchemist more effective in performing the Father's will and in enhancing the value of freedom, let us say unto every man:

The Lord is your shepherd. You shall not

want[4]—if you will only understand that he longs to guide you correctly, if you will only understand that whereas evil has no real existence, its shadowed veil has been the means through the centuries of binding man to the earth. And you shall see that by cutting the bonds of evil and by acknowledging the power of Good, you will no longer strain at a gnat and swallow a camel,[5] but you will enter straightway into the City of God, into the consciousness that transcends the world and its options by recognizing the spiritual options that lie as a gift in your hand.

Man is the Divine Alchemist in physical form. In his right hand the gift of life lies beating. It is the pulsation of cosmic effort. Without acknowledging the gift, man fades away as a vapor upon the glass. By acknowledging it, the cosmic breath strengthens the manifestation of self until death is swallowed up in victory[6] and Life stands forth transcendent and splendid to every eye.

Onward we move progressively toward freedom in action.

I AM

Saint Germain

IV

To Penetrate Matter

To Those Who in Patience Possess Their Souls:

Ere we begin to school the alchemist in more advanced methods of producing the seeming miracles of love manifest right before his eye, we are duty-bound to make further exhortations calculated to prevent the spread of danger through the misuse of higher powers. What do you think the story of the Garden of Eden reveals to man if it does not reveal his disobedience to the divine mandates and his misuse of sacred power?

We will consider then the solidity of substance. Matter that presents so hard an appearance to the eye is actually composed of the whirling energies of Spirit. When the Higher Mind examines the nature of Spirit and makes known its findings to the mind of man, he becomes imbued with what we shall call his first awareness of the potential of the self to penetrate Matter. Matter is no longer solid, but yields to the probing fingers of his mind and spirit. Its density can be calculated and comprehended by the self; and with the speed of light, the consciousness can reach out and pass through dense substance as easily as the swimmer cuts through the water with his arms in motion.

The more the individual becomes aware of the inner power of the self to sense the various shades of reality, the more his powers magnify. At this juncture, the astute and godly man is aware of the need to guard the way of the Tree of Life.[1] Gazing around him upon the world scene, he sees a mixture of good and evil and he knows within himself that in reality you can never blend the two; for whereas black and white may be mixed, their combination will always bring forth a gray tone. In dealing with the human self, man has been convinced over the years that this blending of black and white is the true nature of man. It is almost as though mankind were stigmatized and hypnotized by the concept that the die of sin, like a die that is cast, is itself immutable.

It is to the shattering of this erroneous concept that I dedicate this rendering. Whereas the scriptures of the world are filled with admonishments against sin—and certainly the jangle and discord of the world bears witness to the diabolical inferno that can ignite in the consciousness of man—yet grace and mercy also appear, and beauty, together with the myriad and magnificent qualities of nature. How then shall we distinguish between the darkness and the light as these take shape in mortal consciousness and combine in manifestation?

There are those who argue that the brilliance of the Absolute would lack definition without the tonal values that dilute the pure light into various shades of gray and even black. They say that the darkness is needed as a medium of contrast on which the light can appear. Let me hasten to say that these individuals do not yet have the knowledge that the cosmic law would vouchsafe to them; therefore, let them hold their peace until they know whereof they speak. For they have not considered the introduction of the color spectrum and the emergence of the beautiful pastel hues radiantly functioning in the spiritual world without ever requiring a single shade of gray or black to delineate the many facets of the consciousness of God. Black is the absence of light and of the color-qualities of life, whereas white contains all of the rainbow rays as the prism clearly shows.

Let me say, then, that within the realm of the Absolute, within the goodness of God, within his power to create, lies a chromatic scheme so dazzling and so splendid as to literally propel the consciousness of man out of the socket of mortal vicissitudes. Why then do men and women tarry in the Troys of the denizens of darkness? I say it is through a common ignorance and the unfortunate spread of suspicion and doubt. This distrust of the invisible yet all-powerful spiritual world by men and women is a strange phenomenon, for they are so easily persuaded to give their all in the cause of faithlessness. Contending that God is not and expounding and expanding upon their doubts, they never seem to realize that the energies that they use, if properly directed toward a higher faith, would produce the miracles of alchemy; and these tangible manifestations of the divine power would utterly convince them as to the rightness of the divine plan and ideal.

It has always been inconceivable to the many sincere and religious people that any man would succumb, as Faust did to Mephistopheles, and sell his soul to the forces of nihilism. But this is not so hard to understand if men will recognize that it is possible for faith and doubt to live side by side in

the consciousness of the individual. The presence of
two opposing forces creates vacillation. Therefore
in moments of faith, individuals are able to believe
in the miraculous powers of nature and of alchemy;
but when they allow projections of doubt concerning their own reality to be anchored within
their consciousness, they are able to rationalize
their selfish conduct. Through habit, men use the
energies of God to draw forth the elements of the
good life which they desire. At the same time they
take pleasure in preventing the manifestation of
good in the lives of the innocent and those who may
be far more virtuous than themselves.

Hence we warn of the degradations of witchcraft and black magic. Remember that the goal
of spiritual alchemy is to create nobility in the
soul and virtue everywhere, particularly in the
realm of the self. For how can men extend to the
boundaries of other lives that which they cannot
manifest in their own? Here lies the great error
of the impatient black magician or the advocate
of witchcraft. He is not willing to wait for the
externalization of his own spiritual dedication and
the release of the divine afflatus into the capsule of
identity before exerting his energies on behalf of
controlling the universe.

Now this chapter is the last that I shall write in
this vein. In succeeding ones it is my intent to
release some very interesting keys to the students
of the light. But cosmic law demands that I explain
that the light must always be used to produce the
fervent beauty of dedication to God, love for
humanity, and those divine qualities that enable
the soul to adhere to the tenets of the Great White
Brotherhood. When this is accomplished, we are
certain that we will have not just a few students in
our class on the science of alchemy—or the science

of wondrous change, as our students have come to call it—but we will have many. And these many will also be forewarned and forearmed against the misuse of energy so that all of their earnest efforts will cooperate successfully in achieving the divine plan for the golden age oncoming.

Only the few are aware of the enormous effort being made in the higher reaches of cosmos to assist humanity in awakening from the lethargy of their long sleep in the realm of the human ego—that fantastic and complex forcefield of individuality out of which a god can be born and out of which can emerge monstrous forms of discord and confusion—to the domain of the Real Self that has locked within it, waiting to be released, the greatest secrets of all time.

Today is the Lord's day. Today is the day of the Self. The ages have not marred the power of him who has said, "I AM the same yesterday and today and forever."[2] Therefore, be assured of a kindly response to those efforts which are made in hope, in faith, and in charity; for the greatest masters function in this domain. To be a mortal adept, to move mountains for the sake of greed and the aggrandizement of the human person, is as nothing; for he who has said, "Seek ye first the kingdom of God and his righteousness, and all these things shall be added unto you"[3] meant every word of it.

Right now, today, you stand upon the threshold of fulfillment in your lives as you realize the beauty of nobility so ably stated by Sir Galahad of old: "My strength is as the strength of ten, because my heart is pure."[4]

Let us ready ourselves now for that purity which precedes the greatest alchemical manifestation.

For your advancement and achievement, I
remain

Saint Germain

✠

V

Formulas for Precipitation

To Those Who Can Accept the Challenge to Be:

Not what might be, but what will be because man envisions, invokes, and equates with universal law. Alchemy! The wondrous science of change that fulfills the heart's deepest desires, orders man's affairs, and renews the sweet purity of his original communion with the Great Progenitor.

The concept of the multiplication of cells points to the law of nature that provides for a continual addendum. This law which governs the reproduction of life after its kind does not involve the physical body alone, but the mind, the feelings, and the memory as well as the pure Spirit of man. Coordination between the four lower bodies and the higher vehicles enables man first to control his environment and then to create—on condition that he can understand and not be hindered by the obvious illusions of the appearance world whose point of reference is time and space.

Now the presence or absence of certain factors may either lengthen or shorten the time of precipitation even though all other components be in order. Therefore, when these factors are known, they can be systematically eliminated in order to shorten the time of manifestation. The primary deterrents to precipitation should be recognized as (1) inharmony in the feeling world, (2) a sense of loneliness or abandonment, and (3) a sense of smallness or insecurity and doubt.

Sometimes the presence of these factors can be minimized by a simple act of faith. At other times it may require more earnest application to the Deity and a strengthening of the positive counteractions which are designed to eliminate completely the negative influences manifesting within and without one's world. It may seem strange to some of you that I call to your attention these simple facts; but may I honestly say they are not so simple, for the effects of these mood energies upon the creative intent are of far greater consequence than humanity are willing to admit. By pointing out the need to correct these conditions and making the would-be alchemist aware of the influence they exert upon his desired manifestation, I feel that we are taking a big step in the right direction. For this knowledge applied will avoid the introduction of discouraging factors at a later time when for some the anticipated results will not be immediately forthcoming for the very reasons I have stated.

This brings me to the place where I want to amplify, at the beginning of my instruction, the need for perseverance. Frequently, failure to persevere in the correct course has nullified all fruitage just before the harvest from the invisible world was ready to release itself into the hands and use of the seeker.

We would mention now some of the great and vital alchemical factors whose positive power should also be considered. Chief amongst this list is faith. This includes a belief in the whirling power that keeps the electrons in vital motion revolving around their nucleonic centers. This power resembles a tightly compressed, almost omnipotent spring. It is central to every solar system and atom whose magnetic flux and emanation, while centered in its own nucleus, is able under cosmic law to tie into limitless energy fields to produce whatsoever miraculous manifestation is the requirement of the moment—when the individual is able to convince himself and the universe that his course is right.

Now we have all seen men who were remarkably successful in producing wrong action simply because they were convinced that their course was right, even though they were actually wrong. This does not mean that Cosmos itself is proverbially blind; it is simply indicative of the cosmic need to protect the secrets of creation from the eyes of the curious and to guard the treasures of heaven through the systems of initiation evolved by the Brotherhood. For this very reason the fiat of God went forth "Behold, the man is become as one of us, to know good and evil: and now, lest he put forth his hand and take also of the Tree of Life and eat and live for ever: therefore the Lord God sent him forth from the garden [guard-in] of Eden, to till the ground from whence he was taken."[1]

The inner necessity of the universe to protect its secrets from the profane can be seen in the activities of the luciferian hordes who, from time to time during the long history of the planet, have involved the sons of God in a misuse of the creative and sacred power of life. This they have done through psychedelic perversions, dangerous drugs, their infectious spirit of rebellion against order—

which is heaven's first law—and the spread of chaos, often in the name of idealism. But this brand of idealism has always been based on intellectual pride; it is put forth as the counterplan of the carnal mind that competes with the Divine Mind, considering itself superior thereto. Therefore, if I have seemed overly protective in this intermediate course in alchemy, heaven knows there is a reason for it.

And now I say to each one, taking into account the semantics of alchemy, let us recognize that the word "altar" signifies a sacred place of change. Here all change is wrought by God's law. God is law. His law does not exist without love. But unfortunately, owing to the very generosity inherent within the Divine Nature which allows various functions of the law to be used by evolving humanity, it has been possible for man to separate the law from love.

Thus the more mechanical aspects of alchemy, called magic, have been employed down through the centuries by those who have used their knowledge of God's laws for selfish ends. This was demonstrated at the Court of Pharaoh when Aaron, a true alchemist of the Spirit, was challenged by the magicians who cast down their rods that also became serpents. The mechanical aspects of the law are often combined with trickery to produce phenomena which in the eyes of God are meaningless. Once a man has attained the position of a true spiritual adept, he has developed the powers of love and wisdom within the framework of universal law. He is innocent of harm to any, and his alchemical feats reflect his selflessness. Then the miracles he produces are of far less importance in his own eyes than the miracle of his oneness with his Creator.

So now as we face the altar, the place consecrated to the science of wondrous change, we must recognize the two courses before us. The first is to choose a course of action based on the highest knowledge made known to us. We decide what we wish to change. We decide why it needs to be changed. This gives motive power to our alchemical experiment.

At the same time, we recognize the limitations of man's knowledge and the superiority of the God Self and of the elder brothers of light to assist him in working out his individual destiny. Therefore the second course of action is to be aware that right change can be produced without conscious knowledge of what that change ought to be. We simply invoke from God the purity of his divine plan for right change. In other words, we command in the name of the Lord—which man as a co-creator with God has the right to do—an alchemical precipitation of the gifts and graces of the Spirit that will endow the blessed son with the qualities of the Christ, thereby making him more capable as a spiritual alchemist and more integrated with the universal plan. I have found that wherever the second alchemical technique is employed, it strengthens the first course of invocation (invoked action) and fills the gaps in man's forte of knowledge, covering his ignorance by the cloak of true spirituality.

As we face the altar, aware of the realities of God and of the potential for their realization in man, let us also take into account those masterful beings who have already secured for themselves the ability to produce change at will. Surely the assistance of those who have been successful in the alchemical arts will be invaluable in producing the fruit of our desires. Invocations and prayers of one's choice are then in perfect order. With an awareness of the law, faith in its impersonal operation, and a determined intent that once the formula has been developed the desired manifestation must be released into form, we shall proceed with the business of creating change.

Now one of the most effective means by which change can be produced—and this which I here make known to you is a deep and wondrous secret held by many of the Eastern and Western adepts—is through what I will call "the creation of the cloud." Saint Paul referred to a "cloud of witnesses."[2] I am referring to a cloud of infinite energy which, somewhat like the ether so popularized by the scientists of a century ago, is everywhere present but nowhere manifest until it is called into action.

At first reading, to those who are empirically minded—skilled only in the material aspects of science and in what the senses can perceive—my foregoing remarks may seem to be just so much foolishness. If any think that, I can only have compassion for them. I cannot help them, nor does the law require me to apologize; for I have proved this principle many times with the greatest of success. And I think that where the great adepts do not consciously use it, then it is automated for them through their contact with the Higher Mind. But for most of our beginning and intermediate students, it will be essential that they learn the process carefully in order that they can first consciously create the cloud and then wait until its appearance becomes an automated process in their beings.

I shall continue next week with this very important activity—"Create!" and the cloud.

Onward,

Saint Germain

VI

"Create!" and the Cloud

To Those Who Have Seen the Cloud
  and Are Ready to Create:
    How deeply, how deeply many have yearned
to know how to produce constructive change both in
themselves and in the world. Let them realize,
then, that to bring about change is a creative act.
Alchemy is the creative science whereby man is
enabled to obey the original fiat of God "Take
dominion over the earth!"

    This command was indicative of the Father's
plan for his son, and the means to implement it
are discovered as one learns the ancient secrets of
this sacred science. Practicing the principles of
alchemy, the individual is able to rise from being a
puppet to the will of other egos, to the will of
disobedient spirits, to the passing fancies of the
times, or to the dictates of the brothers of the
shadow who induce the young adept to practice
black magic and witchcraft, flattering his ego and
often quoting scriptures, saying, "If thou be the Son
of God, command that these stones be made
bread."[1]

Now we are on the verge of taking our initial steps in producing change—not a change that gears man to the contemporary scene where his every effort is molded by environmental factors, but a change that will bring him closer to his Real Image. We will create the means whereby change can be produced by our sovereign will, whereby we can take dominion over the earth; for it is here on earth that we are obliged[2] to create the desires of our hearts. It is right here and now that we are indeed obligated to become co-creators with God, thus to fulfill the purity of his intent.

Whereas I recognize that there may seem to be mechanistic factors in the scientific direction that I am about to give you, I am sure you have noticed the many safeguards which I have inserted into this course to make certain that you are never of the wrong opinion; for none should ever assume that by a mere scientific or mechanical ritual he will be able to perform the highest types of alchemical manifestation. Not so! For the highest alchemy, the greatest change, is that which changes man into a god, wherein the son becomes one with the Father; and this can never be accomplished by mechanical means.[3]

Stand now before your altar, honoring the living God and his fiat. For he who is God has commanded it: "Take dominion!" You are rightfully functioning, then, as you do just that. You are about to create, and you will first create the cloud from the enormous power of God stored at every point in space, waiting to be invoked.

The power of vision is central to our invocation. Therefore, we shall create in our minds first a milky white radiance, and we shall see this milky white radiance as an electronic vibratory action of vital, moving, ineffable light. The concentration of the light, which we call the density of the light, is that which makes the milky white color. If the cloud were attenuated, we would be able to see through it as though the scenes around us were enveloped in a fog.

Now, having created in our minds this form of a bright translucent cloud, we allow it to enfold our physical bodies and to occupy our forcefield. For a moment we become lost in the midst of the cloud, and then it seems as though it has always been there. Its atmosphere is familiar, comfortable.

We recognize that the mind has the power to expand its circle of influence, but we must not try to move far from the parent tree of self. Let this bright and shining cloud at first be nine feet in diameter around oneself. Later, perhaps, we shall expand it to a diameter of ninety feet, then nine hundred feet and further.

In our early meditations we shall concentrate on intensifying the action of the white light in our minds. From thence we shall transfer that action to the nine-foot area around the physical form. Once we have developed the sense of this cloud being around our physical forms, we shall understand that whereas the cloud can be made visible to the physical sight, our primary concern is to keep its high vibratory action purely spiritual.

Those of you who are familiar with electronics and the workings of a rheostat will understand that by a simple twist of the dial of consciousness, we can intensify the vibratory action of the cloud. In this case, we coalesce more light around each central point of light; for our cloud is composed of many light points whose auras diffuse and blend with one another, making the total effect one of a lacy yet highly concentrated white radiance, a pure swirling cloud of cosmic energy.

What is this mighty cloud that we have
created, this forcefield of vibrating energy, and
why did we create it in the first place? Actually,
whereas I have used the word "create," it would
be more appropriate if perhaps I used the word
"magnetize"; for we are actually magnetizing
that which is already everywhere present in space.
We are amplifying an intense action of the light
from within its own forcefield—more than would
normally manifest in a given area. We are thereby
drawing upon universal God-power to produce this
cloud that first penetrates and then hallows our
immediate forcefield in order that we may have a
spiritual altar upon which we may project the
pictures of reality that we desire to create.

Bear in mind that this cloud can be used
therapeutically for the healing of the nations and
the soul of a planet, or you can use it as a platform
to invoke, as Christ did upon the Mount of
Transfiguration, the presence of the ascended
masters—of beloved Jesus, Mother Mary, the
Master Serapis Bey from Luxor, the Maha Chohan,
Lord Maitreya, Archangel Michael—to assist you
not only in your alchemical experiments, but also
in your ministrations to life.

Where you are yet ignorant of just what you
ought to produce for yourself and others, you can,
in a gentle childlike manner, ask God to produce
out of the great pool of his light-energy the miracle
of his healing love not only in your life and in
the lives of your loved ones, but also in the lives of
the multitudes in the world at large. You can ask
the power of God and of the kingdom of heaven to
come into manifestation upon earth. You can ask
for the golden age to be born, for an end to strife
and struggle and all negative and hateful manifestations. You can ask for Love to take dominion

over the world. If you will open your heart to the
needs of the world and to the love of the Divine
Mother that seeks expression through your uplifted
consciousness, limitless ideas for universal service
will flow into your mind.

But here again, let me hasten to sound a note
of warning, especially for the benefit of those who
have been psychically inclined or who have a
tendency, as humanity would say, to "go off the
deep end." Beware! You are dealing with sacred
creative power. Beware! It is better for you to ask
the masters to interject their ideas for you—
without necessarily defining or releasing them to
your conscious mind—than for you to be carried
away from the tether of the alchemical norm. The
ascended masters are not only sane and well orga-
nized, but they are also godly and profound to the
nth degree. It is essential, then, that you become
likewise. Above all, be not carried away by pride or
by the exaltation of the self over others.

As you gain spiritual power through these
periods of meditation upon the cloud—which at first
should not exceed fifteen minutes a day—try to
understand that the creative cloud, once it is dispersed by your fiat at the conclusion of your creative ceremony, will continue to expand and expand
and expand throughout the universe as a globe of
translucent white fire, eddying in ever-widening
spheres to contact all that is real and that is really
yours. The cloud, as the manifestation of the power
of your creative energy, the fire of your Spirit, will
draw into your world the very consciousness of God
himself. Evoked from the central pores of being
and beautifully expanding as an altar of God, the
cloud will hallow space wherever it expands.

Christ was able to produce the miracles
recorded in the gospels, and many more, because

he had first mastered the correct use of energy. He called the holy energy of Spirit "Father"; and of a truth, father the Spirit is to all manifestation. The Father is all-loving, all-knowing, and all-powerful; and he will make you all that he is. But we have only begun to touch upon the correct use of his energy. Therefore I seek to develop in your consciousness, through your reading of this material, a proper attitude that will enable you to function, under the guidance of your own God Presence and Christ Self, as an efficient co-creator with God and the Brotherhood of Light.

We need alchemists of the Spirit—men and women who will produce physical, mental, emotional, and etheric alchemical manifestations. Welding them all into one creative act of abundant living, these shall at last understand the meaning of the master's words "I AM come that they might have life and that they might have it more abundantly." [4]

Alchemy is not a devilish means of bringing forth riches and honor. It is a spiritual, all-loving science of changing the base metals that make up the synthetic image of man into the pure gold of the Real Image that he may implement his wise dominion over the earth. Eventually the Great Alchemist will teach the apprentice the seraphic science whereby man shall produce that wondrous final change of which Paul spoke: "Behold, I shew you a mystery; We shall not all sleep, but we shall all be changed, in a moment, in the twinkling of an eye, at the last trump: for the trumpet shall sound, and the dead shall be raised incorruptible, and we shall be changed." [5]

Bear in mind that I have only lightly touched upon this great creative energy that is within you even now.

In the name of the Master of Masters, in the

name of the Lord Christ, I remain his servant and
your advocate forever,

Saint Germain

✠

VII

The Science of Picturization

To Those Whose Gratitude to the Great Alchemist
  Is Expressed in Deeds Well Done:
    Remember that once you have held the vision
of the cloud and turned it over to your Higher Self to
sustain, to the latent God-faculties within you, your
God Presence will sustain it for the required
period. In time you will find that the glow of the
cloud will softly suffuse itself through your physical body, and as this takes place there will come
a sharpening of the mind and a new sense of
awareness of all life everywhere. As you perform
this ritual-exercise of creating the cloud through
attunement with the creative power of the universe, becoming thereby a co-creator with God,
you will gain a feeling of detachment from the
world as though you were merely an observer to
what is taking place around you. This will occur as
you allow yourself to flow automatically into the
great creative power of the Macrocosm.
    This experience in flow, whereby the lesser
consciousness of man flows into the greater consciousness of God, is what is known as "going up

into the mountain."¹ It is called a mountaintop experience because through it man discovers the Summit of his being, the place where the lower self is wed to the Higher, and Matter and Spirit merge. Therefore, throughout this ritual your consciousness must be kept pure, charged with love, aware of the infinite potential of the cosmic mind of God, and completely identified with all constructive momentums. If there is an introduction of hatred or even mild dislike of anyone or an attempt to interfere with the cosmic flow of the infinite plan through any part of life, such activity will, of course, create a karmic situation that will prove most unfortunate to the individual who allows his energies to become so engaged.

Those who have irresponsibly used alchemical techniques, whether in ignorance or with the intent of bringing harm to other lifestreams, have in fact brought about great harm to themselves. Others who harbor feelings of criticism, jealousy, and irritation concerning the actions and accomplishments of friend or foe may create just as much harm as those whose malice is intended. Gossip itself is one of the most deadly forms of black magic and can bring about the physical death of its victims. Seeing that all harm eventually returns to the one sending it forth, would it not be well for all true alchemists to take the vow of harmlessness, at the same time recognizing that the defense of truth and freedom sometimes necessitates making a choice between the lesser of evils?

I urge then that all understand the need to magnetize the grand design of God for all parts of life. Naturally, everyone cannot be expected to be in sympathy with your aims. After all, on the great ladder of souls ascending progressively (hopefully

toward the light of purpose), there are many levels
of attainment. None should condemn those of lesser
understanding or do aught except to emulate those
of greater understanding. Above all, do not be
jealous of those who may be more successful than
you in their application of the science of intermediate alchemy. Remember that it is practice
that makes perfect, that it is motive that trans-
figures design, that it is beauty that transfixes
the soul.

Thus the loving purposes of God come to
fruition in man as He originally intended them to
do, for the Garden of Eden was a place where the
beauty of communion with the Lord and the
understanding of his laws could be imparted to
man. It was intended to be the most beautiful
school in all the world, where the dreams of God
could flow through the branches of the tall trees,
where the billowing clouds of morning, of noon, of
even would be highlighted by the sacred glow of the
luminous sun, "a light to light the day." Lament
not, for the Edenic school shall be reestablished in
this day and age to fulfill the plan of paradise ere
the golden age shall manifest. And it shall appear
when enough alchemists of the Spirit unite in the
common goal of bearing witness to the truth.

Now let us place our attention upon the
science of picturization, for without it nothing shall
appear. You will find this science illustrated in the
story of Jacob, who used alchemy to increase the
numbers of his cattle.[2] Visualization is important to
the alchemist, because it is the overlay of his
visualization upon the creative cloud that actually
produces the miracle of alchemical manifestation.

If you wish a more youthful appearance, you
must visualize yourself as having just that. If you
wish more vitality, you must visualize yourself

already having that vitality—your muscles rippling with God's energy, your mind brimming over with vital ideas, tingling with life and light and love. You must feel and know that the energies of God are flowing through your fingertips and toes, emanating into space the glow of abundant health and a transfiguring countenance.

As you proceed with this exercise, there will be produced, without additional effort on your part, a beneficial effect upon those whom you contact. But you must be very careful not to seek recognition for this service; otherwise, as it is written in the Book of Life, "ye have no reward of your Father which is in heaven."[3]

I know that you will smile when I say that we are aware of some students who, when they are given this material, may become so enthused with it that they will say to those who are uninformed of their efforts to become more godly, "Do you feel something when I am near?" And of course this will spoil the whole effect of any virtue they may have developed during their study. Calling attention to one's accomplishments produces a concentration of energy upon the personality and away from the soul from whence the radiance of the Source is derived. Whereas the inherent God-qualities of the soul are like radioactive substance imbedded in and composing the soul, the radiant cloud is the soul's own alchemical altar which makes possible the soul's expansion—like unto the expanding universe—from the fires of its own central sun out into space.

Some may ask, How can we produce miracles that affect others without taking that energy which belongs to them or without depriving them of the opportunity of producing their own wondrous changes? These seem to be of the opinion that the fires of God have a decay rate and that sometime, somewhere these fires will come to an end or burn themselves out. Let me hasten to assure you that though all of the suns in the physical universe were to fall as burning cinders into the central sun and the central sun by God's law were to be dissolved in its physical manifestation, the fires of the soul of God would never burn out. They are immutable, infinite, and eternal. Have no fear, then, that you are using up God's energies or that you are taking that energy which might be used more profitably by another.

When the fiat "Create!" went forth, it was the signal of God's gift of freedom to man. Therefore, man should be free to create; moreover, he should be free to create without condemnation. To insure his freedom from the impinging thoughts of others, the matrices of his mind must become receptive to and fortified by the thoughts of God and there must be spaces in the time of the day when, apart from the creating of the cloud, the alchemist attunes with the mind of God and drinks in the fragrance of his being.

True alchemy draws man close to God and to his Christ, and it enables him to fulfill the ancient fiats "Man, know thyself!", "Create!", and "Take dominion!" The benefits of man's communion with all life through the sacred science can and will spread abroad throughout the earth. These benefits can and will exert the pressure of the higher techniques of heaven upon the world below.

Have you not read, "Be not forgetful to entertain strangers: for thereby some have entertained angels unawares"?[4] Let men entertain you as angels unawares. Do not sully your alchemical results by imposing the dregs of the human personality upon any man; rather continue in the joyous faith that God will expand and expand and expand the domain of yourself in limitless light and love.

One of the most important points for you to understand in the science of intermediate alchemy is that whereas you are only beginning your training, this is not the only opportunity you will have to use these laws. For you will be able to use them not only all the days of this life, but should you not win your ascension at the close of this embodiment, you will find that so long as you live upon this earth, the science of God's alchemy will help you to be changed "from glory to glory, even as by the Spirit of the Lord."[5] You must understand that there is nothing counter to his law in the correct use of alchemy, for true alchemy *is* the change from glory unto glory by his Spirit.

I know that some who are reading this course may not have considered themselves religious at the beginning. Perhaps the intended functions of the spoilers, the brothers of the shadow, to ruin the purposes of religion by ruining the lives of those who profess to follow religion may have corroded your acceptance of the laws of cosmos. But I think that some of you have already begun to experience profound results in your lives through the practice of the rituals I have given you. And I am certain that those of you who have not will begin to do so as your faith mounts and as you counteract all your negatives by the exhilarating sense that you can change your world and that you can make your life what God wants it to be and what you, deep inside, want it to be. For you can find success in all that you are doing. And that success need not be confined to the spiritual side of life, but it can also include the material.

The Lord has said, "Seek ye first the kingdom

of God and his righteousness; and all these things shall be added unto you." Therefore, fear not to ask that ye may receive of the earthly things that you need even as you have first sought the heavenly. Remember the story of our Lord who, when he would ride into Jerusalem, told two of his disciples to go to a certain village where they would find "a colt tied, whereon never man sat"; they were instructed to fetch "the colt, the foal of an ass,"[6] and to tell those who might question them, "The Lord hath need of him."[7]

Will you develop this sense of knowing that what you have need of, God will supply? Oh, build and build, brothers of light! Build, sisters of light! For God needs you. The kingdom needs you.

Lovingly, I AM

Saint Germain

VIII

What Alchemy Can Mean
to a Decaying World

To Those Who Were Made "in Our Image,
  after Our Likeness":
    The moon rules the night side of life and is the
lesser light, the reflective light of the solar energy
of God. In its reflective state it exerts enormous
control over the tides and over the water element.
Luna, the moon, the great whirling satellite that
rules the night, governs in part then the emotional
body of man and can easily become either his
greatest enemy or his best friend. For when properly harnessed, the energies of the moon (being
put under his feet)[1] can help him to achieve
alchemical control over his emotions (over his
energy-in-motion). Let us see how this is so.
    The moon reflects the astral body of earth.
When dealing with the moon, then, we deal with the
reflected light of the sun. When the astral body
is under the dominion of the Christ, its power
becomes limitless. When its purified energies
are magnified in turn by the moon, which is nothing more than a giant reflector, their power is
multiplied in almost infinite proportion. But until

such time as the mass consciousness is ruled by the
light of the sun instead of being ruled by the night,
the moon will reflect the astral effluvia of the
planet. Thus men will continue to be the victims of
their own horrendous miscreations, and that to an
even greater degree during the cycle of the full
moon.

Now the alchemist uses his purified consciousness as a reflector of solar energies much
like the moon reflects the light of the sun. The
waters of his mind reflect the light of the day and
the night even as the waters of the sea reflect the
golden pathway of both the sun and the moon. But
the Christ consciousness, the prism of purity like
the "sea of glass,"[2] filters out the impurities of the
moon even as it refracts the light of the sun.

All energy being God's energy, the humanly
misqualified energies reflected by the moon (sent
back to the earth from whence they came, according to karmic law) may be freed from the impo-
sitions of the carnal mind through the process of
transmutation. They may then be used to create,
in the tradition of the Great Alchemist, more
perfect works of art until the patterns in the
heavens transform the patterns in the earth and the
moon becomes a golden orb of rarified power.

Most of you know only too well that when your
emotions become disturbed over outer conditions,
feelings, or concepts, there is a moment when you
are yet able to wrest control of your energies
from your own emotional body. Subsequently, if
these energies are permitted to continue to rage
unabated, that moment of control is lost; and then
it is easy for people to do, to think, or to say that
which they will one day regret.

Conversely, most of you are aware of the
great joy and peace that has come to your souls

when you have been able to accomplish something for someone else. This happens because deep within yourself there is a loving desire to serve your fellowman. This desire is what prompted the descent of the Christ, the sun of David, in his role as the Messias of old. The shepherd king, a man after God's own heart, communed with God and prepared himself for greater service as he tended his sheep. Nowhere was the luster of his soul more apparent than in the beauty of his meditations upon the Spirit of the Lord recorded in the Book of Psalms.

One of the most skillful ways in which the tired businessman or executive, the frustrated mother or wife, the confused young man or woman can find integration and wholeness for themselves is to develop the discipline of being able to direct their emotions to do for them exactly what they want. Such discipline will completely change their outlook; for they will then face life with joyous expectancy, not with dissatisfaction.

For example, if it is love for another that you would express, then you must always guard against that love which is selfish, which would exact from the beloved the expectancies of your own mind and heart without ever understanding the givingness of love. In order to love as God loves, you must first give freedom to all parts of life, including yourself; and then you must place your trust, as does a nestling bird, in the heart of God, in the heart of goodness and mercy. Having given all, you will then receive the most joyful, eternal gifts from God that you could ever imagine—and some even beyond that which you could imagine. These will come not only through the chalice of your own heart, but also through the hearts of your compeers. If then you would truly love, you must learn to discipline the base emotions of selfishness, envy, jealousy, resentment, stubbornness, and ingratitude.

We urge therefore at this juncture in our alchemical studies that the control of the emotions be considered, for the emotions will play a very important role in the creative cloud action which we are considering and out of which we are functioning.

The only way to be truly happy is to give oneself totally to the universe and to God, at the same time being aware of and expecting from God the return gift of one's Real Self. One of the greatest dangers in the religious quest has been brought about as men have given themselves to God, thinking that that was all they had to do. Not understanding the responsibilities of free will, they then acted the part of the nebulous ninny. Having no will of their own, they would flip and flop back and forth, blown by every wind, obsessed with what we will call the law of uncertainty. "For if the trumpet give an uncertain sound, who shall prepare himself to the battle?"[3]

Men should understand that although their surrender to God be complete, following surrender they must wait for the fiat of bestowal that is pronounced by the God Presence as a restatement of the blessing given by God at the birth of his offspring: "Thou art my beloved Son: this day have I begotten thee." This takes place when one has relinquished the control of his four lower bodies to his Christ Self, thus enabling his True Self, the Christ, to obey the fiat "Take dominion over the earth!"—the earth being one's own footstool kingdom, the four lower bodies.

Remember that even Jesus the Christ came to the moment of his anointing. The Holy Spirit descended and the voice of God renewed the ancient covenant "This is my beloved Son, in whom I AM well pleased."[4] This is the timeless fiat of creation uttered from the foundation of the world, reconsecrating the soul who has pledged to renew in service his vow taken at inner levels to do the will of God. Therefore, when man's right to function as a son of God is restored, the moment of creativity is born because he has once again recognized the power of God's love to forgive his sins (to set aside his karma until such time as he has gained enough self-mastery to stand, face, and conquer his human creation). Now the bond of life within itself weds him to the highest purposes of alchemy and that, mind you, without ever robbing him of his true identity.

What shall it profit a man if he shall gain the whole world through the use of alchemy and lose his soul?[5] We ask the students to understand that gaining control of the soul (of the energies composing one's identity pattern) is one of the most essential functions of alchemy and that this control is gained through surrender and through humility. When the Christ entered the Holy City riding upon "a colt, the foal of an ass," as we mentioned in our last lesson, his mien was one of utter humility; yet he was crowned by God and man with the highest honors.

And so it is essential that we develop in the students those same Christlike qualities that will make them pillars in the temple of God that cannot be moved by human emotions, no matter what their guise: criticism, condemnation, judgment, self-pity, gossip, treachery, tyranny, or human deceit. The alchemist must be oblivious to all human conduct yet not unaware of worldly thought to the point where he plays the fop. To him the fulfillment of the fiat "Be wise as serpents and harmless as doves!"[6] is the order of every day.

But we are concerned with the sinews of mission, and the mission is freedom for all. If we would have freedom be the joy of all, then we must give freedom to all; for then none can exclude freedom from us. It is therefore to the passions of freedom that our experiments in alchemy must be dedicated. We must rise to emotional control; for when God said, "Take dominion over the earth!" he meant individual dominion over one's energies, one's consciousness, and one's four lower bodies.

Collective dominion comes about when the contributing spirit of the group, the nation, the planet—recognizing all that it has received from life—joyously offers itself and all that it has received to the great Spirit of Life. At that point, man the individual and man the collective unit ponder the enrichment of the Real Self and the true mystical identity of the group through the increase of individual talents. These gifts of God, when multiplied, are like stars in the firmament of being that glow in the grand design of universal destiny.

When man becomes one with God, he realizes that he truly is God. This is not blasphemy, but the fruit of total surrender. The return gift of life's own identity, as God gives himself to his son, is far greater than the token sacrifice of mortality left on the altar by the beloved son. Nevertheless, it is typical of the Deity to be the Great Giver and thus to precipitate the highest alchemical manifestation—the prism of the Christ consciousness. This must be and always is the reward for the relinquishment of human error and the full realization of the divine life in every man.

All nature then trembles within the cup of the Christ mind. The heart of the Christ is brimming with the creative essence which pours out the unifying experience that identifies him with life, him with the alchemist, and the alchemist with him. Who can hurt or destroy in all my holy mountain?[7] Who can aid in all the holy mountain of God? Why, every atom, every electron, is a rushing unto God!

"And a cloud received him out of their sight...Ye men of Galilee, why stand ye gazing up into heaven? this same Jesus, which is taken up from you into heaven, shall so come in like manner as ye have seen him go into heaven."[8] The Second Coming of Christ is antedated by the fulfillment of the prophecy "One shall be taken, and the other left."[9] For when one is taken and another is left, it denotes that the world lieth yet in wickedness and that only the few have accepted the kingdom. But when the Second Coming of Christ comes to the quickened world, it will be because the nature of the Divine has become understood as a priceless gift of freedom to every man.

When this miracle of Christ-love is produced in the world, it will be because the students of alchemy—whether known by that name or any other, whether in the churches or out of the churches, in fact whether in the body or out of the body[10]—are expressing universally the radiance of the Christ-design. Imbued with the fires of the Holy Spirit, their minds will then become a cosmic reactor, a central furnace of universal ideas for freedom and for the breaking of the chains of bondage that a recalcitrant humanity have forged.

Now we reveal in this eighth lesson what alchemy can mean to a decaying world, what it can mean to slaves in bondage to the senses, what it can mean to the self surrounded by confusion and chaos as it becomes an ordered, purposeful exhibit of universal grace expressing through the forcefield of the individual identity of man.

Do you see now why El Morya and Mother Mary and all of the ascended masters are offering their energies freely for the good of humanity? Do you see why the creative cloud invoked by us, literally an individualized cloud of witness by day and a pillar of fire by night,[11] enables man to understand that the crucible of identity, while it may at first be nothing but an experimental test tube, can become a radiant altar of reality?

Faithfully, I AM

Saint Germain

✠

IX

Anxiety and the Anxiety Syndrome

.

Friends of the Great Alchemist:

For this lesson we will permit the students to experiment with and develop proficiency in the creation of the cloud while we go afield for a moment to discuss one of the major deterrents to successful alchemy. I refer to anxiety and the anxiety syndrome.

Strange as it may seem, most negative manifestations stem from anxiety, including the awful sin of masochism.[1] Since it is generally acknowledged that humanity have a desire to be happy and that they have the right to pursue happiness, we ask this question: Would it not be wise for people in all walks of life to work toward the healing of those conditions which they bring upon themselves through their unfruitful anxieties?

We avow that there are lawful concerns and that men and women should make reasonable provision for their future and for eventualities which they know from personal experience may arise. But it is so unnecessary for them to become apprehensive about life in general, or even life specifically, to the point where their apprehensions unbalance their thinking, their emotions, and their entire psyche.

Anxiety is the great warp of life. It warps perspective without producing any perceptible benefit whatsoever. Anxiety is the cause of people's tendency to hoard the goods of this world; like frantic squirrels they pile up their winter's supply of nuts. They accumulate an oversupply of every imaginable item, and they deprive themselves of happiness by their unwarranted concerns and their unnecessary and time-consuming preparations for every eventuality.

Just as we do not expect that the students will cease to be providential, so we do not expect that they will become unduly involved in anticipating a doomsday that never arrives. Anxiety is a symptom of insecurity; it stems from man's incorrect concept of himself and from his lack of perspective. Many people feel unfulfilled, unloved, unwanted, and they are not sure of just what they should be doing with their lives. Their uncertainties under adverse conditions are easily turned into mental and emotional states of depression bordering on extreme self-deprecation.

Considering these facts and bearing fully in mind the power of creative energy, we have decided that before going more deeply into our study of alchemy, we shall advocate for all of our students an utter mental, emotional, and even physical catharsis. We shall achieve thereby a purification of the consciousness and being of man—an emptying, if you will, of unstable conditions so that our alchemical creation may take place under the most sterile and clinical conditions possible.

You see, it is so easy for a negative ingredient to creep into our formulae that we must take every possible precaution before we begin our experiments. Without first purging ourselves of all undesirable qualities, we would find ourselves, with the best of motives, amplifying our negatives instead of our positives as we proceeded to employ the wondrous power of alchemy.

This is one of the problems that arise among those who follow some of the so-called mystery schools where the ego is catered to at the personal level instead of being disciplined at the impersonal level. As these students develop "soul power," it is inevitable that they amplify their negative momentums along with the great positive qualities which they seek to manifest. For whatever is in their worlds when they are brought into direct contact with the sacred fire must expand even as their total consciousness expands.

In some cases the negatives completely cancel out the positives; and many times, because of earthly affinities, the additional boost of power that comes about as the result of experimentation will make a magnet out of their negatives even when they are completely involved in the divine search. Thus will their own negative momentums, hidden in the recesses of their subconscious minds, draw to themselves more of their kind from the thoughts and feelings of others. This phenomenon is often the underlying cause of disharmony in religious groups.

Now we earnestly desire to have the body of God upon earth forewarned about these conditions, for unless the deterrent forces which are imbedded in the psyche of man are brought under the power of divine grace and emptied of their content (i.e., of the misqualified energies which sustain their

forms), they will peer as haunting specters waiting to devour the offspring of all benign activities
and to literally turn man's light into darkness.

We would do the opposite. We would create in
the lives of the would-be alchemists the transmutative effects that will enable them, through
awareness and through dedication to the Christ
Spirit of living harmony, to manifest all good
things under divine control. Thus shall divine grace
fill the temple of the mind and heart of the
alchemist and make him truly a wonder-worker for
God.

How many times have we seen concern for his
fellowman take shape in the consciousness of the
student. As he gazes upon world conditions or upon
the problems of his own family, he is often almost
obsessed with the desire to produce the miracle of
saving grace for his loved ones as well as for those
who are in need in the world around him. So strong
does this desire become that his brotherly love is
many times the central motivation behind his
search for greater spirituality and self-realization.

Ours is not to discourage those who would
serve, but to help them realize their objectives in
peace and in honor. Therefore, "consider the lilies
of the field...they toil not, neither do they spin: and
yet I say unto you that even Solomon in all his glory
was not arrayed like one of these."² The care of God
for the birds of the air, the great abundance
manifest in nature and in the "lilies of the field,"
shows the supreme value that God places upon
each of his children. Let us look to him, then, to
teach us how to meet the needs of our brethren here
below.

Anxiety stems from a lack of faith in the
ultimate purposes of life. The hard experiences
that have come to many in childhood and in later

years, creating stresses and strains and producing the fruit of bitterness, have prevented their development of that refined spirit which would enable them to shed their anxieties. In reality, the lessons Jesus taught on the Father's watchful care for man and nature should give all the understanding that will heal their insecurity, their anxiety, and their personal pain involving the mind and self. This healing is brought about through the overpowering radiance of God's loving concern for every man.

I urge therefore that all students take into account the tender care and consideration of the universe manifest in the wondrous working of the physical body when it is not interfered with by human pollutants. And I urge that they then make an attempt throughout the coming days to heal the breach caused by their sense of separation—the separation of the individual from his true identity and hence from the Eternal One.

In him you live and move and have your being. Without him you have neither life nor identity. Ask yourself this question: Is it wise for you to pollute the Divine Identity by the intrusions of self-will and self-indulgence? Ask yourself this question: Have you really given the Father a chance or has yours been an on-again, off-again, vacillating attempt to realize God? There is nothing complex about the origin of the soul and its everlasting communion with him. To become as a little child, then, as we shall see in our next lesson, is to prepare the way for the greatest manifestations of alchemy.

Now alchemy is not witchcraft; it is not variance. It is the exercise of a stable God-intended control over nature, and it involves far more than men imagine. Through alchemy the shedding of your anxieties can be accomplished, but first you must build a mountain of faith to counteract the negative thoughts of the world which are primarily responsible for man's failures. How is this so?

Each time individuals have a failure and lament it, each time they have a problem and sorrow over it rather than commit it unto the Father, each time individuals resent their problems and see them not as the return of karma or as a test but as an act of Deity whom they defy, they are building up in their own worlds frustration, resentment, anxiety, and confusion. And these momentums draw to their own doorsteps the negative conditions of the outside world.

If ever there was a secondary enemy to anxiety, it is confusion. This, too, can and should be healed by the fires of the Christ mind. For we know that the Christ mind is calm yet capable of focusing the fiery energies of the Creator to overthrow evil both in the self and in society. But let us make clear that this is a fire whose burning is controlled by the mind. It can be slow or fast; it can leap like a young deer and take its freedom, its dominion, its God-control, or it can stand in mid-air like hieroglyphs of living flame and say to all that would hinder the alchemical manifestation, Pass no further!

I urge you to consider then the negative thought pools of the world with a view to disengaging your energies and your activities from involvement with the misqualified energies contained therein. And I urge you to make your God-determination that you are going to clean your consciousness inside and out of all residual substance which is there as the result of your contact with the cesspools of human consciousness.

Anxiety must go. It must be replaced by faith and solemn confidence in the outworking of the divine plan. This certain knowing, I say, is a happy state! When you begin to understand fully what I mean, you will see that the developing of this confidence in the real is one of the greatest ways in which all deterrents to successful alchemy can be vanquished. In fact, all deterrents to abundant living can be knocked down as you cease to fight "as one that beateth the air,"[3] as Saint Paul once said.

You were born to win, and I say this to counter the lie that man was "born to lose." And if you will make this statement, "I AM born to win!" as an act of supreme faith, it will overcome the world's consciousness of failure—a deadly weight of sin if there ever was one.

It does not matter what problems you have faced, for even the most dire situations will yield to the mighty forcefield of God-potency that will be built up through your practice of spiritual alchemy. But why should man draw God's energies for alchemical experimentation and creation when his own world is still full of the miscreations of the mass mind and the weeds in his garden that will choke out his efforts and destroy the good fruit as well?

I do not mean that you should not continue your experiments with the cloud. I do mean that you should understand the duality of life and realize that anxieties must go. But in order for this to take place, you must make the conscious determination that it shall be done. And if you do, I promise you that your experiments will not only be purer and more successful, but also that they will produce happiness and the fruits thereof for yourself and the whole human race.

Oh, we have so much more, for each master loves each servant-son!

For freedom to all, I remain

Saint Germain

X

Nature Yields to the Childlike Mind

To Those Who Are Willing to Become
  as Little Children for the Sake of Alchemy:
    The most important key we can release to the
alchemist at this stage of his development is found
in these words of Jesus: "Whosoever shall not
receive the kingdom of God as a little child shall in
no wise enter therein."[1] All of the pristine beauties
of nature—the ethereal highlights whose gentle
glow can be sensed by the budding spiritual
faculties of the children of God—hold as their
essential content the sweet creative longing of a
child.
    I do not wish to disabuse the minds of the
children of men who have held such high and
mighty opinions of the masters of cosmos of any
false glamour with which they have clothed our
office under the Godhead, almost as a gilding of the
cosmic lily. However, I do feel the need to point out,
not only from my own experience but also from the
experiences of those who are above me in the
hierarchy, that the higher we have gone in our
contact with the Deity, the more childlike, the more

simple, the more beautiful has been his represen-
tation.

Therefore we conclude that the innocence of
Nature herself is perhaps the greatest key to her
potential for wondrous alchemical creations. We
amplify then the need of the children of God to
empty their minds of the dregs of turbulent emotions that have engaged their energies through
the centuries and kept them bound to a senseless
round of confusion and struggle. The great barrier
to spiritual progress has been that men confuse
holy innocence and becoming like a little child with
playing the fool. The highest masters are childlike,
sweet, and innocent. Nevertheless, when functioning in the world domain, they sharpen their
"worldly senses" in order to execute judgment in
human affairs.

The reason I introduce the subject of becoming "as a little child" into our study of intermediate alchemy is that every factor of thought
and feeling impresses itself upon the sensitive
matrices of alchemical manifestation. No thought
or feeling, then, can be termed unimportant or
irrelevant. Without hesitation, I declare that the
most important of all alchemical factors in drawing forth the highest aspects of creation is the
childlike mind—pure and guileless.

The child mind is the greatest mind because
its innocence is its best and sure defense, because
it is not surrounded by crowding concepts, and
because it is free to develop symmetry, color,
sound, light, and new ideas. In short, it is free to
create; and its supreme goal is to spread happiness
in all of its forms and manifestations, all the while
maintaining the purity and harmlessness of the
child.

Let me say, however, that the idea of harmlessness is applicable only to the world of human beings, for how can there be a need for harmlessness unless there first exist harm? When you destroy harm, you no longer have need to create harmlessness. In the absence of harm or harmlessness, the innocence of childhood prevails, enabling the souls of men to commune gently with nature and nature's God.

The vast drama that keeps the way of the Tree of Life, that guards the alchemical secrets, has also been born of necessity. Man's disobedience to cosmic law, his hesitancy in matters of the Spirit, his gathering momentums of destructivity upon earth—these have necessitated the curbing of his activities in heaven. In a very real sense, then, man has been confined to the earth to work out his destiny. Eden, the Garden of God, and the secrets of life contained therein have been denied him because he would not heed the divine injunction "In the day that thou eatest thereof thou shalt surely die!"[2]

Now and always man must understand that when he partakes of the consciousness of evil, he becomes subject unto the laws of mortality. Yet God has always been ready to receive him again as a little child. The compassion of the Christ toward those who had lost their innocence was apparent in his lamentation "O Jerusalem, Jerusalem, thou that killest the prophets, and stonest them which are sent unto thee, how often would I have gathered thy children together, even as a hen gathereth her chickens under her wings, and ye would not!"[3] We come therefore before the court of innocence, and we plead for a communication to humanity of the flames of purity, truth, and cosmic innocence.

Among the greatest misconceptions that have ever been formed in the minds of men is that which concerns the nature of spiritual realms. Men either think that heaven is remote, unfulfilling, and lacking in the joys of this world, or they imagine that it is the ultimate goal—the reward of the faithful and their relief from the oppressions of a world of sin, a place where they will have nothing further to do and all progress will cease. In both cases the fallacy is in thinking that the future will bring man something that is not available to him today. Life is abundant—here, now, and forever. Wherever you are, it needs only to be tapped.

May I say then that I have walked and talked with the elder gods of the race. I have met with the greatest interplanetary masters, cosmic and angelic beings. I have attended ceremonies in the grand halls of the retreats and strolled the cosmic highways. In short, I have had the most wondrous experiences since my ascension, and with me still is the memory of all of my earthly experiences prior to my ascension. But none of these are worthy—even the highest of them—to be compared with the experiences I have had in the mind of the Divine Manchild. Thus should the alchemist realize that neither heaven nor earth can give him that which he has not already found within himself.

Truly, "eye hath not seen, nor ear heard, neither have entered into the heart of man, the things which God hath prepared for them that love him."[4] What a pity that more cannot shed this false sense of a far-off and future good! The secrets of life are to be found here below as above. The changing of base metals into gold would produce only earthly beauty and earthly wealth. But the changing of the base nature of man into the refined gold of the Spirit enables him not only to master the world of the Spirit, but also to take dominion over the material world.

If all power in heaven and earth is given unto me,[5] then I can give it to whomsoever I will. Yet would I will to give it to those who would abuse and misuse it to the hurt and harm of their brothers? Why was the flaming sword placed at the east of Eden?[6] Why was the continuity of existence interrupted by death? Why did illness, warfare, and brutality flash forth and take hold in human consciousness? Why was anger sustained? Was it not because people have been afraid of loss—loss of self-respect, loss of individuality, loss of relativity? Actually, what have they to lose? Nothing but their fears, nothing but their negatives. For that which is tethered to reality can never be lost.

Let men learn to empty themselves completely of their attachments to the earth; so shall they begin to enter into the childlike mind and spirit of creative innocence. The greatest angels who keep the way of the Tree of Life cannot deny those who have reunited with the wholly innocent mind of God access to Eden. How can they then deny it to the Divine Alchemist in man, who in honor reaches forth to take the fruit of the Tree of Life that he may indeed live forever?

The meaning of the allegory is quite simple. So long as man lives according to the "earth, earthy," according to the concepts of "flesh and blood,"[7] he cannot inherit the kingdom of heaven, he cannot sustain the heavenly consciousness. But when in childlike innocence he enters into the divine domain, he finds that all of the universe is his; for now he belongs to all of the universe.

This sweet surrender to the mighty currents of cosmic law and purity shows him the need to transfer from the higher octaves of light into the lower ramifications of self the power and the glory, the victory and the overcoming, the transmittal and the transmutation. He must shed the glitter and the glamour; he must replace it by light and purity and do all things well. He must seek for the spirit of excellence; he must forget limitations and all things that are behind. He must have faith in that which he cannot yet see and know that Nature herself holds a cornucopia of loveliness and light waiting to be showered upon him when the magic word is spoken.

How beautiful then is the cloud—the cloud of witness. But how important are harmlessness and simplicity. How towering is faith! How gentle! Sweet yet mighty is the faith that moves mountains.

Because we are approaching a time of greater discovery, I have carefully prepared the mind and consciousness of the students for the most beautiful experiences in the world, but I have not kept them confined to the domain of temporal life. I am creating in you states of inner awareness that will assist you in evolving spiritually, whereby, even if the body were shed, the mind of the Holy Spirit would flow through you and teach you the way of the Christ, the way of the helper, the way of innocence, and the way of happiness.

Humanity are bored, they are frustrated, they are ungentle. Through what you would call the "hoopla" of life, they have taken on the phoniness that the dark powers have created, spread abroad, and popularized as worldly sophistication—the antithesis of the childlike consciousness. "Ye are the salt of the earth: but if the salt have lost his savour, wherewith shall it be salted?"[8] We reiterate the master's statement because it reminds us that the essential flavor of living is in the cultivation of the inner sense of beauty and reality.

That which you receive from God is never denied to anyone; they only deny it to themselves in their ignorance. We all have a responsibility to encourage the light to expand in all people, but each one must open the door for himself. Each one must enter into the realization that the Divine Redeemer is the Divine Creator and that since man's descent into the lower octaves of human consciousness, the Lord of Light has continued to emanate his radiance everywhere.

He is available yet hidden.
He is real, yet cloaked with unrealities
By the minds of men and their life experiences.
He is light sometimes covered over
With the darkness of men's misqualifications.
He is the Great Supplier
Of every good and perfect thing.
He combines the green shoot and the crystal snow.
He combines the ethereal in the sky that glows
With fiery sun from solar center.
His loving heart bids all to enter:
"Take upon you, precious child,
Garments of mastery, meek and mild.
Dominion need not bluster,
Yet dominion e'er shall muster
Each required grace
To help the world keep pace
With cosmic legions when facing senile moments.[9]
Youth and light appear when facing time's election.
Shed then all your fears and glow,
Eternal fires of youthful cosmic innocence!"[10]

On the brink of discovery, we remain your faithful teachers of light and divine alchemy.

Saint Germain

XI

The Highest Alchemy

To Those Who Have Disciplined Their Minds
to See the Cloud:

The sense of reality and the sense of delight
with which the student aspiring to create concen-
trates upon the cloud determines its efficacy. In
alchemy, as in all things, doubt and negation
destroy; faith and happiness sustain.

Man must come to recognize that space and
time are necessary subdivisions of one sole reality,
that the limitations which they embody, providing
necessary boundaries, can become ladders to
boundlessness and a veritable means whereby any
electron in space can become a universe or the
universe can become any electron. The drawing-in
of the sustaining breath of the Holy Spirit and
the expelling thereof creates an eddying of consciousness in concentric, rapidly moving rings
expanding out to the farthest periphery of manifestation.

The finite mind may find it difficult at first to
grasp this principle. To make it easier, let us
explain that the consciousness of God that sustains

the universe is also within man. Now if the consciousness of God that sustains the universe is within man, is it unreasonable to suppose that man can also be within the consciousness that sustains the universe?

In the macrocosmic-microcosmic interchange, in the great flow of life, of delight, of boundless joy, man senses the unity of all that lives; and he recognizes that his role as a receiver of benefits from the universe entails the necessary conveyance of benefits from his own creative consciousness back into the universe. There is joy in the construction of the temple of life; for templed order and templed service create in the individual a sense of building when all around him there is a tearing down of values, morals, and faith. But in the temple he finds his constructive role midst the roles of destructivity men have elected for themselves.

Many say, "Let us destruct that we may construct." Let them remember that before they can construct wisely and rightly, all destructive tendencies must be removed from their consciousness; for creative law, as it expands the reality of God into the framework of the natural order, automatically wipes out their imperfect images.

There is no need to hold in consciousness a destructive sense or even a sense of condemnation. Beloved Jesus said, "For God sent not his Son into the world to condemn the world, but that the world through him might be saved."[1] The secret of the Tree of Life is to be found, but the seeker must first surrender his personal sense, his sense of separation from God and from life, so that the universal consciousness can flow into him. Thus the breath of the Great Alchemist shall become his own.

It is not then the personal "I" that doeth the work, but the Father in me that worketh hitherto, and I work.[2] The Father that worketh hitherto is the creative effort of the universe that enhances the vision of life's perfection for an onward-moving humanity. The "I" that works is the conscious individuality yoked with the I AM Presence of universal reality. It is the Son working with the All-Father to produce in and for every man the summation of the glory we knew together before the world was.

If imperfect manifestations defraud the functions of cosmic law, then let it also be remembered that Spirit enhances the quality of life. Through the beautiful bonus of man's acceptance of the reality and the flow of life, he becomes wholly identified with the formless Spirit. He is then able in the form manifestation to create a relative perfection as above, so below.

As the great Master admonished his disciples, "Be ye therefore perfect, even as your Father which is in heaven is perfect,"[3] so we would disabuse the minds of the would-be alchemists of the idea that form cannot be perfected within a relative framework. While we acknowledge that according to the patterns of evolution forms and ideas do transcend themselves in life's great cosmic ongoing, we also see that within a transcendental universe scientists have been able to perfect their methods and inventions through the historical epochs. Thus the dispensations of science have been ordained in the hopes that in relieving mankind of their drudgery, they would use their free time and energy to develop the Christ consciousness that overshadows and transcends the mortal mind and being of man.

The Great White Brotherhood is aware of how destructive trends in music and art can exert enormous influence on young minds. Many of the youth of today have no standard by which to judge that which is fed to them, simply because from early years they have been enmeshed in a web of darkness which seems to them to be a creation of light. It becomes difficult, then, to extend the wings of the Spirit to these young souls; for the human intellect inciting their rebellious egos has convinced them that free form and the absence of all restrictions is the means through which they will achieve self-realization. Nothing could be further from the truth, for self-discipline is the requirement of the hour. But these untamed souls would not surrender their human will for anything or anyone, and so it is easy for the prince of darkness to find disciples from among those who have been subverted from their earliest years.

The highest alchemy is the precipitation of the Christ consciousness, and all to whom the breath of life has been given have a solemn obligation to pass on the precepts of holy wisdom before passing the torch of responsibility to the next generation. The ancient proverb "Train up a child in the way he should go: and when he is old, he will not depart from it" becomes then life's injunction to all humanity. Seeking a means of improving the strain and the quality of life, they should consider and reconsider its mandates until they are effectively interwoven into the whole structure of striving toward the future.

Immorality, greed, selfishness, and dishonor have never provided for any age any recompense except the destruction of the spirals of the future. Only light can rise, whether in civilization or in individual man. Only light has the power to endow our cloud with the understanding that it is our own future, woven today from the controlled energies of our beings and determinedly endowed with our highest vision and our richest faith, that will produce the fruit of givingness to the universe in the highest creative God-quality.

As I prepare you for more advanced efforts made on your behalf and on behalf of humanity, it is essential that I endow you to the best of my ability through spiritual means with the vision of what God is. Even in our higher octaves, it is impossible for us who are yet in a lesser individualized state to realize the fullness of who and what the Greatest Alchemist is. But we can approach the holy of holies; we can draw nigh by transcending ourselves even as he is ever transcending himself, being changed from glory unto glory by the one universal Spirit.

We are never bored and never tired by the changeless effort to change; for we are aware that with each step we take, an infinite leap occurs in the highness of us all. God identifies so beautifully with every part of life that there is a gladness in all creation when the Higher Self makes the giant leap. In the words of the Christ to his disciples of old, "I go before you into Jerusalem."[4]

The City of God, the City of Peace, the cosmic parliament of man—these are the outgrowth of the Father's love, of the idea of the Great Transcendentalist, of the Eternal Alchemist, the Great Spirit, God the Father, Christ the King. He who brings down the mountains and raises the valleys, he who puts down the mighty from their seats and exalts them of low degree,[5] does all things in order to produce the *summum bonum* of ultimate reality for every part of life.

His givingness is beyond reproach; and if his precepts had been heeded in any age by any society, the thorns of that age would have been blunted and broken. The fragrances of the rose

would have surrounded the age. The highest
learning, culture, and beauty would have man-
ifested. Pain and suffering would have ended
in a relative sense and, through understanding, the
golden arch would have been seen by all within the
scope of their immediate realization. The golden
door would have ope'd wide, and the heart of
purpose would have been perceived behind it all.

Nature and nature's God conspire to produce
universes worlds without end, the great diurnal
magnetism, the universal endowment that, as male
and female, as positive and negative, as Spirit and
Mater,[6] are designed to produce the wonder of
life. Its glaring and awesome beauty may be
everywhere, but to some it is a garish movement
from which they shrink. To others it is a universal
hymn of purpose. But to those of us who love
nothing more dearly than to guide humanity by
word and deed, it is the opportunity of the eternal
Buddha, the opening bud of the flower of joyous
reality whose fragrance is everywhere. It per-
meates the quality of life; it removes the odors
of darkness; it encompasses all. It reveals the
meaning and purpose of love that in sacrificing
itself is reborn. What more shall I say as we stand
on the threshold? I say, I kindle a blaze within your
being. Be the flame tiny or great, may it ever
expand and help you to make for yourself and for
the glory of the Great Alchemist a life full of
interest in taking dominion and in being one with
the Great Exemplar.

Oh, let us love together! Let us be together,
and let us see together the far-off movement that
yearns to draw nigh.

Graciously, I remain

Saint Germain

XII

The Way of the Tree of Life

My Friends Who Have Determined
  Never to Be without the Cloud:
      The fervor we seek to convey can be assimilated. The fire of our mind and spirit can be absorbed through a simple reading and application of the consciousness, of the heart. We know that man can inductively enter into a higher state. The sincere reading and rereading of our words until they become a very part of the consciousness of the disciple-aspirant can and does create in him a key by which his own alchemical expertise is developed.

      So much interest has developed in many of you concerning the creation of the cloud that I wish to expound still further upon it. The cloud is the means whereby man alters his destiny. I do not say that there are not other methods that can effectively achieve this purpose. Each karmic act has its own recompense. Each deed that men do, each thought that they think makes its imprint upon their lives. But many of these are negatively qualified, hence destructively manifest. They come haphazardly through experiences which men do not govern; for when men do not govern their worlds, they are governed by the circumstances of the world. Through the creation of the cloud, then, we seek to transcend time, space, and even karma— short-circuiting many of the old spirals, shortening the time of man's realization of his own God-reality,[1] and helping him to realize in an avant-garde manner the graciousness of the Lord of the Universe.

There are many schools of the Brotherhood. There are many methods of achieving. In our releases through The Summit Lighthouse, we seek to assist our students in expanding their consciousness with facility. We seek to weld together the body of God upon earth by first creating the understanding of both the beauty and the practicality of true alchemy. We are not interested in forming a society of magicians who will go around producing seeming miracles—albeit we acknowledge that the proficient alchemist, even through this course, can do just that.

What we are interested in is the subscribing of our students to a universal brotherhood and body already existing spiritually as the Great White Brotherhood. Being in the invisible, this order, comprising the alchemists of the Spirit, requires a union with embodied humanity. For only through this association can we formulate the most beautiful sustaining concepts that will enable the entire house of the world to breathe the air of freedom and to be infused with the fires of destiny in its individual and collective aspects.

Man must see and know that as he is and as he does, so others see and do. Thus in perception and in action, man can endow the pages of history with a revelatory illumination, thereby fulfilling the fiats of God "Take dominion over the earth!" and "Set the example for the age!" With each act of grace, man becomes endowed with more grace. Each step of self-mastery raises him higher in the cosmic peerage, until he is crowned at last through the eternal mysteries with the full realization of his own potential.

Our cloud, then, in answer to some of your questions, can become physically tangible. It need not be so in order to endow you with the highest graces. Through the cloud you can draw to yourselves God's holy witnesses that have lived in all generations, that have called him blessed, that he has blessed. You can be freed through the light and fire of the cloud from the mediocrity of the present age and from the degradations of past ages and their cumulative effects upon the human psyche. You can, as it were, rend the veil of the holy of holies if your purpose be communion with the Most High, as was Moses' in the Sinai Desert. You can realize through the cloud the full perfection of your glorious I AM Presence.

Then through your contact with the I AM Presence, the Presence of all being, you can develop a culture of the Spirit at lower levels that will provide stairways of safety upon which others may climb. There is never any need, regardless of what outer manifestations or vile astral energies may seek entrance to your world, to yield to these depredations. You have the power of the Christ to cast out unwanted states of consciousness.[2] The Great Alchemist lives within you. You live within him. Therefore, through your conscious experimentations with the cloud, you can surround yourself with the means of producing change.

In our examinations of those who through the ages have worked with the cloud, we have taken note that those who have been convinced of the reality of the cloud, those who have dared to endow their consciousness and being with the very qualities of the cloud itself, have become more and more efficient in its use. For them each daily experiment in creating change has become easier.

I hope that I have conveyed to you, in this intermediate course, the ideas I have sought to convey. Please understand, however, that the full power and glory can only unfold within the concepts of the total course. It is my hope, as it was to create this series when I first produced *Studies in Alchemy,* to one day produce for you *Advanced Studies in Alchemy.* We shall then be able to offer humanity a beautiful trilogy—the first section laying the groundwork of ideas[3] through the golden flame of illumination, the second herein pronouncing the love ray that through the cloud of the Holy Spirit endows your ideas with life, and the third section explaining how to make permanent that which you create through the power of the spoken word. This trilogy will be especially valuable to those who are not only concerned with "magick," but who also recognize that alchemy is the means of renewing youth, first in the inward parts of man and then throughout his entire consciousness and manifestation. And if this be accomplished, it cannot help but be the means of enhancing individual and world thought.

Now as you ponder the correct experiment for your efforts in alchemy, remember that the stereotypes that abound in the world are not all ugly. In fact, there are many historical and cultural literary masterpieces that embody divine stereotypes, or archetypes as we would call them. It is not necessary for the student in his alchemical experiments to shun all that appears to be of the ordinary. In many cases, rather than ferret out the commonplace, it is more important that you avoid the classification of a condition as trite; for in reality it may be a great idea. Do not fear to embrace beautiful thoughts because someone else thought of them first. The time will come when you will develop a greater uniqueness. But until you become more proficient with your experiments, it is more important that you go upon a safe highway; that is, if speed combined with exactitude be your desire.

There comes a time when man passes beyond the pale of that which his own experience patterns can teach him. Then the immortals stand ready, even as they do while he is still learning the lessons of earth, to help him expand in every facet of his endeavors, whether human or divine. Progress is never governed as much by what man desires to do or to be, or even by what the world has to offer, as it is by his realization that he can be all that God wants him to be, if he will just accept that simple thought.

Seek not then the bizarre; rather be content to be a good man or a good woman. Place yourself in the hands of God, in the hands of the Father of all, who cares for the birds of the air and the fragile flowers that glow for the breath of a moment. Do you not think that he cares more for you than for the grass of the field that withereth away—he who esteems you enough to give you his consciousness, to create for you a universe, a universal Mother, Nature herself, and to impregnate that nature with the fires of his own Spirit—all for you, all for you? Yet man is as the grass of the field[4] when he esteems himself so to be, when in mediocrity, self-ishness, deceit, and a sense of personal struggle, he strives only for outer recognition.

Let men seek not to be thought great of other men, but to recognize internally the greatness of God that is inherent in all of life's manifestations. Then their alchemy will hold within it the alchemy of becoming perfected. I do not say there are not other great mysteries waiting to be revealed in connection with alchemy. I know that there are. I do say that

> The way of the Tree of Life
> Which is the perfect secret
> That God has guarded from the curious
>   and profane
> Remains a penetrable mystery
> To him who is not ashamed
> To wear his wings,
> To him who understands
> The diligence of each day,
> To him who is content to place his hand
> In loving trust that destiny is ours,
> To him who is willing to forsake
> A past that has not produced
> The blossoming beauty he craves,
> To him whose heart reaches up as a cup
> To the highest and sweetest,
> The noblest and best Lord of all
> In the desire to have imparted to himself
> And every part of life
> The best of gifts.
> He speaks in summoned, loving tones
> Of inward communion,
> "O Father, not my will but thine be done!"
> To him there is conveyed the highest crown,
> The word "dominion."
> He is the Son, the Alchemist,
> The beloved one.

He can divide the loaves and fishes,[5]
Walk upon the waves,[6]
Fulfill his own and others' wishes,
And be the Great Benefactor.
In him the Immortal Spirit prevails,
The ultima Thule is seen.

I sign myself sincerely, your immortal friend,

Saint Germain

✠

Camelot. This lovely 218-acre paradise reminiscent of King Arthur's island-valley of Avalon is home for Church Universal and Triumphant. Here, nestled in a secluded valley of the Santa Monica Mountains on one of the most picturesque campuses of Southern California just a few miles from Malibu beaches, you will find the cradle of the Coming Revolution in Higher Consciousness. Return to nature—the true nature of your soul—at Camelot. Here students of Summit University and Montessori International prepare to challenge and reverse trends of Antichrist directed against the liberation of souls everywhere. We have chosen to call our home Camelot because we believe that with God's help individuals dedicated to freedom and enlightenment can forge a better world. The name symbolizes a community of men and women taking responsibility for self-government. To them, the quest for the Holy Grail means a lifetime of love, sacrifice, and disciplined effort in defense of truth, honor, and the four sacred freedoms of the sons and daughters of God. The teachings of the ascended masters of East and West form the foundation for the rebuilding of Camelot today.

Incarnations of the Ascended Master
Saint Germain

SAINT GERMAIN as Samuel the Prophet, of the tribe of Levi, priest and initiator of the prophetic order in Israel. His life is recorded in the book of I Samuel (eleventh century B.C.), beginning with the story of Hannah, wife of Elkanah. According to the tradition of the law, Hannah accompanied her husband each year to the house of the Lord at Shiloh where she prayed earnestly and wept because she was barren. After many years of sorrow and supplication, Hannah made a vow before the Most High that if she would bear a son, "I will give him unto the Lord all the days of his life." And so it is written that "the Lord remembered her" and she brought forth a son and called him Samuel (meaning "his name is God") "because I have asked him of the Lord."

As soon as the child was weaned, Hannah took him to the temple as she had promised and presented him to Eli, the priest. Even as a child, Samuel ministered in the temple before Eli, for his sons "were sons of Belial; they knew not the Lord." Once while Samuel was sleeping, the Lord called to him. Thinking that it was Eli who spoke, Samuel went to the priest and answered, "Here am I," but Eli said, "I called not" and sent him away. "Now Samuel did not yet know the Lord, neither was the word of the Lord yet revealed unto him." Again and still a third time, Samuel was called by name until Eli "perceived that the Lord had called the child" and told him how to answer. "And the Lord came, and stood, and called as at other times, 'Samuel, Samuel.'" Then Samuel answered, "'Speak; for thy servant heareth.'" So God spoke to him concerning Eli and his sons: "For I have told him that I will judge his house for ever for the iniquity which he knoweth; because his sons made themselves vile, and he restrained them not." And so it is written that "Samuel grew, and the Lord was with him...and all Israel from Dan even to Beersheba knew that Samuel was established to be a prophet of the Lord." At that time, Israel went against the Philistines and when they were overcome in battle they said among themselves, "Wherefore hath the Lord smitten us today before the Philistines? Let us fetch the ark of the covenant of the Lord out of Shiloh." So they took the ark to their camp and "all Israel shouted with a great shout." Now the Philistines heard the cry and they understood that the ark of the Lord was with the Israelites and they were afraid, saying, "God is come into the camp." And so they fought with great determination and defeated Israel, slaughtered 30,000 men, and captured the ark of

the covenant. Then it is written that "the glory is departed from
Israel: for the ark of God is taken." But wherever the ark was
held, the people witnessed disease and destruction and so it is
written that "the men of Kirjathjearim came and fetched up the
ark of the Lord...And it came to pass...that the time was long;
for it was twenty years: and all the house of Israel lamented
after the Lord." Samuel spoke to the people of Israel, telling
them that if they returned to the worship of the one God, He
would deliver them from the continual attack of the Philistines.
"Then the children of Israel did put away Baalim and Ashtaroth,
and served the Lord only" and as Samuel had prophesied the
Philistines were subdued, Israel regained her lost territories,
and there was a lasting peace. "Samuel judged Israel all the
days of his life," traveling extensively throughout the land. But
as time went on, he grew old and the people of Israel rose up and
demanded of him a king "to judge us like all the nations."
Samuel was troubled at this and prayed to the Lord who answered him saying, "They have not rejected thee, but they have
rejected me, that I should not reign over them." Despite the solemn warnings of Samuel as to the arrogant oppression of kings,
the people were insistent. And so God sent Saul, a Benjamite,
into the city where Samuel was prepared by the Lord to receive
him as king. After Samuel anointed Saul with oil, he sent him
into the company of prophets so that "the Spirit of the Lord will
come upon thee, and thou shalt prophesy with them." Then he
gathered together the people of Israel and showed them the king
whom God had chosen. And "Samuel called unto the Lord; and
the Lord sent thunder and rain that day: and all the people
greatly feared the Lord and Samuel." Now "the ark of God was
at that time with the children of Israel," and "there was sore
war against the Philistines all the days of Saul." But when he
was called of God to "go and smite Amalek and utterly destroy
all that they have," Saul was disobedient and spared the best of
the spoils. So God spoke to Samuel and said, "It repenteth me
that I have set up Saul to be king...And it grieved Samuel; and
he cried unto the Lord all night." Samuel went and spoke to Saul
and rebuked him saying, "Rebellion is as the sin of witchcraft,
and stubbornness is as iniquity and idolatry. Because thou hast
rejected the word of the Lord, he hath also rejected thee from
being king." Through Samuel, the Lord appointed David in his
stead. Saul became fiercely jealous and sought to kill David.
Therefore David fled to Samuel's house at Ramah and abode
with him until the prophet's death. Now the Philistines again
gathered their army against the people of Israel and after Saul
saw the strength of the enemy he was afraid, but "when Saul en-
quired of the Lord, the Lord answered him not." So he went to
the witch of En-dor that she might call Samuel up from the

grave to speak to him. And Samuel himself came from inner
planes to reproach Saul saying, "Why hast thou disquieted me,
to bring me up?" And Saul told him "I am sore distressed; for
the Philistines make war against me, and God is departed from
me, and answereth me no more." And Samuel said unto him,
"The Lord is departed from thee...because thou obeyedst not
the voice of the Lord." And he prophesied to him that "the Lord
will also deliver Israel with thee into the hand of the Philistines:
and tomorrow shalt thou and thy sons be with me." And so it
came to pass at Mount Gilboa that Saul was slain, and "there
was long war between the house of Saul and the house of David:
but David waxed stronger and stronger, and the house of Saul
waxed weaker and weaker.... Then came all the tribes of Israel
to David unto Hebron, and spake, saying, Behold, we are thy
bone and thy flesh," and the elders of Israel anointed him king.
"And David went on, and grew great, and the Lord God of hosts
was with him."

SAINT GERMAIN as Joseph, chosen by God as the protector of
Jesus and Mary. Joseph was of the house of David, a descendant
of the greatest kings of the tribe of Judah and the most illustri-
ous of the ancient patriarchs. Much of his life with Mary and
Jesus is recorded in apocryphal writings. According to Matthew's Gospel of the Birth of Mary, she was three years of age
when her parents, Anna and Joachim, presented her at the temple at Jerusalem to be raised by temple virgins. When Mary was
fourteen years old the high priest made a public order that all
temple virgins "as they were now of a proper maturity should
according to the custom of their country endeavour to be married. To which command, though all the other virgins readily
yielded obedience, Mary the Virgin of the Lord alone answered
that she could not comply with it. Assigning these reasons, that
both she and her parents had devoted her to the service of the
Lord and besides that she had vowed virginity to the Lord, which
vow she was resolved never to break." The priest, being per-
plexed, commanded "that at the approaching feast all the principal persons both of Jerusalem and the neighbouring places
should meet together that he might have their advice, how he
had best proceed in so difficult a case. When they were accord-
ingly met, they unanimously agreed to seek the Lord and ask
counsel from Him on this matter. And when they were all engaged in prayer, the high priest, according to the usual way,
went to consult God. And immediately there was a voice from
the ark and the mercy seat which all present heard, that it must
be inquired or sought out by a prophecy of Isaiah to whom the
Virgin should be given and be betrothed; for Isaiah saith, there
shall come forth a rod out of the stem of Jesse, and a flower shall

spring out of its root, and the Spirit of the Lord shall rest upon him, the Spirit of Wisdom and Understanding, the Spirit of Counsel and Might, the Spirit of Knowledge and Piety, and the Spirit of the Fear of the Lord shall fill him. Then, according to this prophecy, he appointed that all the men of the house and family of David who were marriageable and not married should bring their several rods to the altar, and out of whatsoever person's rod after it was brought, a flower should bud forth and on the top of it the Spirit of the Lord should sit in the appearance of a dove, he should be the man to whom the Virgin should be given and be betrothed." But Matthew tells us that Joseph, being advanced in years, "drew back his rod when every one besides presented his. So that when nothing appeared agreeable to the heavenly voice, the high priest judged it proper to consult God again, who answered that he to whom the Virgin was to be betrothed was the only person of those who were brought together who had not brought his rod. Joseph therefore was betrayed. For when he did bring his rod and a dove coming from heaven perched upon the top of it, everyone plainly saw that the Virgin was to be betrothed to him." Then while Mary was living in Nazareth and Joseph, her betrothed husband, was "building houses abroad, which was his trade," Archangel Gabriel appeared to her and announced the birth of Jesus. It is to blessed Joseph that we are indebted for the preservation of the life of the infant Saviour when Herod sent forth the command for the slaughter of the holy innocents. For "behold, the angel of the Lord appeareth to Joseph in a dream, saying, Arise, and take the young child and his mother, and flee into Egypt, and be thou there until I bring thee word." (Matt. 2:13) Now Egypt was to them "a foreign, unknown country, without help or acquaintance" according to St. Crysostom. It is recorded in the apocryphal Gospel of the Infancy of Jesus Christ that when the holy family arrived in Egypt, the "country trembled" and the idols fell to the ground. Jesus performed many miracles while in Egypt those three years. And "when Herod was dead, behold, an angel of the Lord appeareth in a dream to Joseph in Egypt, saying, Arise, and take the young child and his mother, and go into the land of Israel: for they are dead which sought the young child's life. And he arose, and took the young child and his mother, and came into the land of Israel." (Matt. 2:19-21) Then the holy family returned to Nazareth, where Jesus served with Joseph as an apprentice, his first wood carvings setting the example of the Father principle and the mastery of the masculine ray. According to the Gospel of the Infancy, "Joseph, wheresoever he went in the city, took the Lord Jesus with him, where he was sent for to work to make gates, or milk-pails, or sieves, or boxes; the Lord Jesus was with him wheresoever he went.... On a certain time the King of Jerusalem sent for him, and said, I would have thee make me a throne of the same dimensions with that place in which I commonly sit. Joseph obeyed, and forthwith began the work, and continued two years in the king's palace before he finished it. And when he came to fix it in its place, he found it wanted two spans on each side of the appointed measure.... Jesus said to him, Fear not, neither be cast down; do thou lay hold on one side of the throne, and I will the other, and we will bring it to its just dimensions. And when Joseph had done as the Lord Jesus said, and each of them had with strength drawn his side, the throne obeyed, and was brought to the proper dimensions of the place." It is believed that Joseph passed on before the miracle at Cana, with Jesus and Mary at his side to comfort him. For this reason, Christians throughout the world pray to St. Joseph for solace in that hour. St. Joseph is called the Saviour of Egypt, for it was through his intercession that the people of that country were once preserved from great famine. St. Teresa chose St. Joseph the chief patron of her order. Of him, she says, "I do not remember ever to have asked of God anything by him which I did not obtain." The feast of St. Joseph is celebrated on March 19.

SAINT GERMAIN as St. Alban. Although the faith of Jesus Christ was brought to England during the time of the apostles, it was not until the third century that Roman persecution began in that country, probably during the terrifying reign of emperor Diocletian. St. Alban was the first of the Christian martyrs of Britain. Alban himself was a pagan who served in the army in Rome for seven years. Upon returning to his homeland, he met with Amphibalus, a fugitive priest who appeared at his door seeking refuge from Roman soldiers who demanded his life. Alban admitted him into his home and was so edified by the holiness of the stranger that he inquired into the tenets of his faith. As Amphibalus related the story of his own conversion, Alban's heart was opened to divine grace and he was filled with love for the Saviour and an immediate understanding of his word. After several days, a report was given to the Roman governor that Amphibalus, a renowned evangelist, was with Alban and thus a warrant was issued for his arrest. Perceiving the intent of the soldiers who soon arrived at his home, Alban exchanged clothes with Amphibalus so that the famed teacher might escape to carry the message of Christ far and wide throughout Britain. Wearing the robe of the priest, Alban presented himself to the soldiers who bound him and led him away. The judge recognized Alban and, outraged at his trickery, proceeded to deal with him even more cruelly than he would have Amphibalus himself. Alban was dragged before the pagan idols, scourged, and mercilessly tortured before being sentenced to death. In the bliss of his communion with God, Alban watched as a multitude gathered and went out ahead of him to witness his execution. As they came upon a narrow bridge, Alban saw that the great crowd would not be able to pass over it before the day's end. And so he walked before them to the riverbank. There, in the spirit of the prophets of Israel, he lifted up his eyes to heaven and prayed to the Lord God who only a few days before was unknown to him. The stream was miraculously divided to afford passage for Alban and a thousand followers. The executioner was converted at once and fell down at the feet of Alban, begging the opportunity to die in his stead. Both Alban and his supposed executioner were beheaded on that day and their example did much to further the cause of Christendom in England. And so it was that Saint Germain took incarnation as a pagan in order to play a role in this drama. A church was built in honor of St. Alban on the place of his martyrdom in c. 793. A monastery was subsequently added and around it the present city of St. Albans gradually grew up. The feast of St. Alban is celebrated on June 22.

SAINT GERMAIN as Proclus (410-485), Greek philosopher of the fifth century, a brilliant student of the elders at Alexandria and later a favorite pupil of Plutarch. Proclus became the highly honored *diadochus* or "successor" of Plato as head of the Platonic Academy at Athens where he taught metaphysics. He is known as a great systematizer, expositor, and commentator and it is through him that Neoplatonistic ideals reached their fullest development and spread throughout the Byzantine and Islamic worlds. His numerous works include *Elements in Theology* and *Elements in Physics*.

SAINT GERMAIN as Merlin the Magician first appears in the history of England prior to the birth of Arthur as mediator among barons and war lords during the sixth century. Like that of Arthur, Launcelot, and Guenevere, his story is recorded in the folk tales of nearly every European nation. According to Thomas Malory's account *Le Morte d'Arthur*, Merlin stands highly revered as the king's counselor, at times appearing disguised—once "all befurred in black sheepskins and a great pair of boots"—in order to convey the imminent message, warning, or initiation. According to Malory, Arthur was born to Uther Pendragon, "king of all England," and noble Queen Igraine at Merlin's own bidding with the understanding that the child would be delivered to Merlin as soon as he was born. And so the tiny newborn babe bound in a cloth of gold was brought to the "poor man" at the postern gate of the castle and taken to Sir Ector whose wife nourished him at her own breast. Merlin

The Ascended Masters Jesus and Saint Germain

The Ascended Masters Jesus and Saint Germain, passing the torch of the Christ consciousness and the I AM THAT I AM for the Piscean and Aquarian dispensations, stand in the long history of the earth and her evolutions as the great deliverers of nations and peoples by the sacred fire of freedom and the salvation of the soul through the path of the ascension. This is the path of initiation that leads to the soul's reunion with the I AM Presence through the mediator, the Christ Self—the open door of the eternal Christos which no man can shut—personified in the Christ flame of the Piscean Master Jesus. It is the path of initiation by the baptism of the sacred fire of the Holy Ghost revealed through the God consciousness of the Aquarian Master Saint Germain as he delivers to the people of God the dispensation of the seventh age and the seventh ray—the violet flame and its invocation through Father, Son, and Holy Spirit.

Saint Germain is the seventh angel prophesied in Revelation 10:7 who comes to sponsor the finishing of the mystery of God "as he hath declared to his servants the prophets." Saint Germain brings to the lost sheep of the house of Israel the remembrance of the name of the Lord God— I AM THAT I AM. This ascended master, who was embodied as the prophet Samuel, calls the Twelve Tribes from the four corners of the earth and makes known to them their true identity as the light-bearers commissioned to serve with the Ancient of Days to set the captives free by the Christ Self, their own Real Self—the Word that was the true light which lighteth every man that cometh into the world.

Jesus and Saint Germain, together with all of the heavenly hosts, ascended masters, Elohim, and archangels—the Spirit of the Great White Brotherhood—have come forth in this moment of the turning of the cycles of Pisces and Aquarius to teach us how to call upon the name of the Lord in order that we may overcome the dragon, the personification of evil, the *e-veil,* or *energy veil,* referred to in the scriptures as the carnal mind, the Devil, the Evil One, the Adversary, Lucifer, Satan, etc.

This great overcoming of the darkness by the light was prophesied by Jesus Christ to his disciple John as he wrote in the Book of Revelation: and they overcame him "by the blood of the Lamb, and by the word of their testimony." The blood of the Lamb is the essence, or "Spirit," of Christ which is his teaching withheld from the people for thousands of years by 'false Christs' and 'false prophets', now brought forth once again by the ascended masters and their messengers. The "word of their testimony" is the science of the spoken Word whereby through prayer, meditation, dynamic decrees, and communion with the Lord, his sons and daughters become the instrument of his Word as the fiat of the Logos.

Thus the knowledge of the true teaching of Christ—now brought to our remembrance, as Jesus promised, by the Holy Spirit in the person of the ascended masters as they release their dictations to the messengers— combined with the decrees of the Lord God, the I AM THAT I AM, spoken through the ascended masters and their unascended disciples, are the means whereby the light-bearers overcome the world tyranny of the fallen ones in this and every century. This Great Overcoming following the "Great Tribulation" is decreed by Almighty God as is the coming of the ascended masters, their messengers, and their disciples. It is the teaching and the mission of the Ascended Masters Jesus and Saint Germain that we must make every decree of the Lord our own and then stand fast to behold the salvation of our God.

As the deliverer of both Jew and Christian from the leaven—false doctrine of the Pharisees, ancient and modern—Jesus and Saint Germain

The Ascended Master Jesus Christ

The "Anointed One," World Saviour, World Teacher, Hierarch and Avatar of the Piscean Age; Great Exemplar of the Second Person of the Trinity and Personification of the Only Begotten Son of God; the Open Door to the Christ Consciousness Individualized as the Light, the Christ Self, of Every Child of God, Serving on the Sixth Ray (purple and gold) of Ministration and Service; Wayshower of Sons and Daughters of the Word Incarnate; Initiator of Souls on the Thirty-Three Steps of the Path of the Ascension

The Ascended Master Saint Germain

Chohan (Lord) of the Seventh Ray, Hierarch of the Aquarian Age, God of Freedom to the Earth, Sponsor of the United States of America, Great Alchemist and Dramatist of the Soul's Evolution through the Planes of Time and Space into the Great Sphere of Cosmic Consciousness, Initiator of Souls in the Science and Ritual of Transmutation through the Violet Flame of the Holy Spirit proclaim the Messiah already come in the threefold flame of each one's heart and in Jesus who as the Son of God came to teach us the way of the Christ, personified not in himself alone but in every son and daughter of God. Thus in truth, and in the true science of the religion he taught, all mankind can and shall declare with the blessed Sons of God "I AM the way, the truth, and the life" and understand that it is the I AM THAT I AM, the Lord our God, dwelling in our own temple who is, was, and forevermore shall be the way, the truth, and the life.

The likenesses of Jesus and Saint Germain were painted by Charles Sindelar, famous American artist and illustrator of the 1920s and '30s. Jesus Christ appeared to the artist on twenty-two consecutive mornings at 2:00 a.m., and the image of the Master would appear throughout the day over both canvas and etching plate, distracting him from his work until he took the advice of a friend to "paint what you have seen." After five days of continuous work, the portrait was completed. Charles Sindelar was not satisfied with his rendering of the mouth and therefore on the fifth night at 2:00 a.m., Jesus returned until the artist had perfected on canvas the likeness of his master who stood before him.

The messengers testify that the portrait of Jesus is the exact likeness of the master as he has appeared to them both in the retreats of the Brotherhood, in their homes, and on the platform during dictations. They have confirmed that the portrait of Jesus depicts him as he appeared at the Royal Teton Retreat "in consultation with Saint Germain and the tall master from Venus."

A number of years after the painting of Jesus was completed, Saint Germain appeared to Charles Sindelar in the presence of Guy Ballard, and the artist completed the portrait as the messenger served as the anchor point to sustain the forcefield and the Electronic Presence of Saint Germain. Again the messengers have stated that this likeness of Saint Germain is indeed that of the ascended master who is their sponsor and the sponsor of America and every nation on earth. He has been known to devotees of freedom on the planet Earth for over seventy thousand years, and his great love and sacrifice has enabled the evolutions of earth to have the use of the violet flame for the transmutation of all misqualified energies of the human consciousness which stand between the soul and its salvation, *Self-elevation,* through the Christ personified in Jesus, the Saviour, the fullness of the Word incarnate.

The Ascended Masters Jesus and Saint Germain have given their life and their likenesses in these paintings as a glad, free gift for the salvation of earth and her evolutions and "that the earth may be filled with the glory of God as the waters cover the sea." Neither the masters nor their portraits can be confined to any creed, religion, doctrine, or dogma, nor can their names be invoked for the sealing of anyone's private interpretation of the law or the scriptures.

These blessed ascended masters are the intimate friend, guide, teacher, counselor, and comforter on the way of life, walking hand in hand with the light-bearers in this age. All who will call upon them in the name of the I AM THAT I AM will be blessed with an immediate manifestation of their Electronic Presence—the fullness of their tangible light body focalized in time and space within the aura of their disciple. The devotee may visualize himself with his right hand in the hand of Jesus and his left in the hand of Saint Germain. Calling upon these great wayshowers of the Twelve Tribes of Israel, devotees of truth may know with the certainty of cosmic law, whereby the call compels the answer, that these ascended masters will never leave him as long as he remains obedient to the principles and practice of Truth, Life, and Love, to the Law of the One, and to the inner God Flame, the I AM THAT I AM.

called a holy man to christen him and named the child Arthur. Within two years, while King Uther lay mortally ill, his enemies "did a great battle upon his men and slew many of his people." Merlin bade the king to ride into the battlefield on a stretcher, for "if your person be there...then shall ye have the victory." So it was at St. Albans that Uther's men overcame the "great host of the North." The dying king returned to London where Merlin called together all the barons of Uther's realm in order that the king might name his heir. And Merlin said aloud, "'Shall your son Arthur be king after your days?'" And Uther answered, "'I give him God's blessing and mine'...wherewith he yielded up the ghost." The land of England stood then "in jeopardy a long while," for many rose up attempting to capture the crown by force. So Merlin went before the Archbishop of Canterbury and counseled him to call all the lords of the realm to London at Christmas in order that Jesus, born King of Kings, might come to show who should rule England. By the alchemy of the Christ consciousness, Merlin caused the sword and the stone to appear in the churchyard of Canterbury cathedral with these words: "Whosoever pulleth out this sword of this stone and anvil, is rightwise king born of all England." By the trial of the sword—representing the power of the soul that is free from the bondage of attachment to things material symbolized by the stone and anvil—Arthur proved his kingship. Thereafter, Merlin remained at Arthur's side as counselor and friend. The young king once would have died by the sword of mighty Pellinore had not Merlin appeared and "cast an enchantment" upon the knight. It was because Arthur's sword was smitten in two during that fierce joust that Merlin and Arthur rode to the lake where they miraculously beheld rising from the water the arm of the Lady of the Lake holding the magnificent sword Excalibur. And Merlin later counseled him, "Look ye keep well the scabbard of Excalibur for ye shall lose no blood while ye have the scabbard upon you" —a prediction well fulfilled in future years. It was Merlin who went before King Leodegrance to announce the desire of Arthur to wed his daughter Guenevere. He returned triumphantly to Camelot with Lady Guenevere and the Round Table, a gift to Leodegrance from Arthur's father, Uther Pendragon. Merlin revealed the mystery of the blessed Sangreal (Holy Grail) to king and queen, knights and ladies at Camelot and, early in Arthur's reign, prophesied the day of the "great battle beside Salisbury and Modred his own son would be against him." It is told by Malory that in the end Merlin was "bewitched" and shut under a stone by one to whom he had entrusted his alchemical secrets.

SAINT GERMAIN as Roger Bacon (c. 1214-1294), English philosopher and experimental scientist. Bacon belonged to a wealthy family, was educated at Oxford, and later became a Franciscan monk. While living at the monastery in Paris, Roger Bacon began his research of "secret" books and the construction of experimental laboratories. From 1247 to 1257, he devoted himself entirely to an exhaustive investigation of alchemy, optics, and mathematics, as well as a thorough study of languages and astronomy. He once remarked that the zeal with which he pursued his scientific research was talked about everywhere. Due to his vigorous activity and obvious impatience with those who refused to understand his work, Bacon was brought under severe discipline by his Franciscan superiors. He appealed to Pope Clement IV, however, who requested Bacon to inform him of his projects. In a remarkably short time, Roger Bacon produced *Opus Majus, Opus Minus,* and *Opus Tertium*—a vast encyclopedia of all the known sciences, including his unique understanding of alchemy and methods of experimental study. Bacon's doctrine embraced the Trinity as the threefold nature of divine revelation: the Word, the works of nature, and the inner illumination of the soul achieved through seven stages of "internal experience." At the same time, he defined three invaluable assists to the interpretation of the message: the mastery of languages, the knowledge of mathematics, moral and spiritual disciplines. Wisdom is fulfilled, however, only through "experimental science," which Bacon describes as application of theory to practical life—useful discoveries and inventions as well as "good works" necessary for the perfection of the soul. He insisted upon the knowledge of linguistics for adequate comprehension of Scripture, wrote a comprehensive Greek grammar, and was relentless in his attack of corrupt translations of the Bible. Bacon's genius lies in his extraordinary ability to correlate science and religion. His unique insight led him to see the magnifying properties of convex lenses, the inherent power in gunpowder, and the possibility of aircraft. Many of Roger Bacon's works were written in a secret cipher. Sometime between 1277 and 1279, Bacon was imprisoned by fellow Franciscans because of "novelties" in his teachings. His condemnation was largely due to his lively critique of theologians and scholars of the day as well as his credulity in matters of alchemy and astrology. His pioneering in the realm of experimental science has won him the title Doctor Mirabilis (Teacher of Wonders).

SAINT GERMAIN as Christopher Columbus, Cristóbal Cólon (c. 1451-1506), the discoverer of America aptly named after Saint Christopher, who by legend is pictured carrying the infant Jesus across the waters. His surname means "repopulator." Christopher Columbus was born in Genoa and as a young man studied astronomy, geometry, and cosmography at the University of

Pavia. At age fourteen, he was already a skilled seaman. While employed as a mapmaker in Porto Santo in 1479, Columbus was privileged to examine charts of the Portuguese explorers who endeavored to find a sea route to the Orient by sailing southward along the unexplored African seacoast. Some of these documents were at that time a state secret. In addition, he pored over the *Book* of Marco Polo, the *Imago Mundi* of Pierre d'Ailly, the logs and records carefully kept by his deceased father-in-law who had served as naval captain under Henry the Navigator. Columbus was often seen engaged in hearty conversation with old seamen and sailors returning from African voyages. Step by step, he conceived the idea that the world is a sphere. His daring proposal for a westerly voyage to the East Indies as finally developed and presented before the courts of Portugal and Spain was supported by theories of geographers, reports of mariners, and actual evidence of unknown civilizations that from time to time washed ashore. Unlike most of the fortune-hunters of the age, seamen and kings alike, Columbus was deeply religious and sought passage by sea to the Orient not only for her wealth but also for the firm establishment of Christianity among the Asiatics. Columbus first presented his carefully charted plans to John II of Portugal who turned the matter over to a body of distinguished scholars. Although they concluded that his proposal was "unrealistic," the king favored the theory and secretly dispatched a caravel of his own. The sailors soon returned, however, disheartened and afraid. When Columbus discovered the treachery he departed for Spain, arriving in 1484 during a fierce war between Christians and Moors. King Ferdinand and Queen Isabella were preoccupied with their military struggle and therefore unable to give due consideration to Columbus' proposals. Year after year he waited, meanwhile taking the issue before Henry VII of England and Charles VIII of France, but to no avail. It was not until January 2, 1492, that the war ended and Columbus received an audience with the queen. The plan was flatly rejected, however, after Columbus impetuously demanded the rank of "Admiral of the Ocean," vice royalty of all lands he found, and ten percent of the precious metals he might discover. On his way out of the country, Columbus went to Luis de Santangel, the king's treasurer, and announced his discovery of the northeasterly trade winds which would safely and surely carry him across the uncharted seas. Santangel then went to Isabella and convinced her of the vast importance of the mission. The queen immediately dispatched a messenger who found Columbus already on the road for France. Isabella met with him and hasty preparations for the voyage began. With eighty-eight skilled, but skeptical sailors and three nearly inadequate ships, Columbus and his crew set sail for the

New World the morning of August 3, 1492, after receiving Holy Communion. Long weeks at sea failed to produce sight of the land the admiral had expected (Columbus had correctly defined the shape of the earth but grossly underestimated its size). It was an age of superstition, and common fears included everything from sea monsters to falling off the "edge" of the world. Ascended Master Saint Germain himself has described how he quelled violent mutiny aboard his ships during that first voyage. Finally at ten o'clock the night of October 11, 1492, Christopher Columbus first sighted land, pointing out a dim light ahead. The next morning he landed, richly clad and accompanied by his captains bearing banners of the Green Cross. When they all had "given thanks to God, kneeling upon the shore, and kissed the ground with tears of joy, for the great mercy received," Columbus named the island San Salvador and took solemn possession of it. At the same time, the crew who had shown themselves doubtful and mutinous sought his pardon, weeping and prostrating themselves at his feet. When the natives (called "Indians" because Columbus believed he had reached the East Indies) told him tales of the plentiful gold to be found in neighboring lands, Columbus set sail in search of the treasure and for a fortnight wandered among the lovely islands. It was then that he discovered Cuba, magnetized by the violet-flame focus of Lord Zadkiel's retreat. While further exploring the area on Christmas night, 1492, the Santa Maria drifted into a reef. When the natives of nearby San Domingo came out to rescue the men, Columbus observed their rich ornaments and believed that his search for a land of gold was ended. There he founded his first colony, La Navidad, and built a fort from the remains of the sunken ship, placing its crew of forty-four in charge. On January 4, 1493, Columbus and the remaining men departed for home. Along the way, they encountered a violent storm which quickly subsided after the crew implored the assistance of Mother Mary and drew lots to see who would make a pilgrimage to her shrines. On March 4, the Nina dropped anchor off Palos. Columbus proceeded to Barcelona in a sort of triumphal procession and was received by the king and queen in full court where he related his fantastic story. A second expedition was immediately prepared to secure and extend discoveries already made. The new party set sail on September 28. Upon his return to La Navidad, Columbus found that one third of the 300,000 inhabitants of the island had been killed in struggles between Indians and Spaniards. Columbus restored partial peace with the Indians who had been unjustly treated, rebuilt the fort, and proceeded to explore the islands from Cuba to Jamaica. During this time, however, he became exhausted by the physical and mental strain of his expeditions. In these trying times, he wrote in his journal that he was thirty-three days practically without sleep. Columbus lay ill for five months, during which time he entered into deep communion with God. Thereafter, he was met by a royal commission who acted in harsh judgment of his administration. Columbus, dressed as a Franciscan, was sent home in 1496 but was cordially received by his sovereigns. In 1502 he appealed for a third voyage and was quickly granted support. Returning to La Navidad, he again found that affairs had not prospered well in his absence, and so displeasing were the reports now brought before Ferdinand and Isabella by returning colonists that the king and queen appointed a royal representative to take Columbus' charge. He stood accused of severity, injustice, even of venality and was finally shipped back to Spain, bound in chains as a criminal. In the meantime, however, Queen Isabella had received a heartbroken and indignant letter written by Columbus to an associate, explaining the events in La Navidad in his own terms. Upon counsel with his majesties, the admiral's property and office was restored. During his fourth voyage, Columbus' ships ran aground in a small inlet on the island of Jamaica. Columbus and his crew were received with great kindness by the natives, who provided them with food for more than a year while they awaited assistance. After that time, the admiral suffered much from disease and from the lawlessness of his crew, who incited mutiny and alienated the natives, provoking them to withhold customary supplies. Columbus restored their trust by "miraculously" predicting the eclipse of the moon thereby proving his favor with heavenly powers. Upon his safe return to Spain, Columbus was again well received, although his health was rapidly failing. He passed on in May 1506, uttering the words: "Father, into thy hands I commend my spirit."

SAINT GERMAIN as Francis Bacon (1561-1626), Lord Chancellor of England, statesman, essayist, the "father of inductive science." His contemporaries believed that he was the son of Sir Nicholas Bacon, Keeper of the Great Seal of England during the reign of Elizabeth I. In the nineteenth century, however, the complete story of his life began to unfold when the first volumes of the famed "Bacon-Shakespeare controversy" appeared and Francis Bacon emerged as the brilliant author whose sonnets, poems, and plays still remain the most cherished of all English literature. The idea that the "Shakespearean" plays were not the work of William Shakespeare has been the subject of scores of books, first based on the obvious disparity between the magnificent work and the somewhat obscure character of Shakespeare—a common actor with insufficient learning, the son of a small provincial tradesman at Stratford-on-Avon. In contrast, the plays exhibit the genius of one with extensive education in language and literature, thorough knowledge of law, history, and politics, firsthand experience in the high courts of Europe, and unquestioning familiarity with the manners and speech of royalty—requirements so aptly met by Lord Bacon. Following another less speculative method of investigation, literary scholars late in the century discovered within the "Shakespearean" works a strange and secret tragedy—a drama within a drama—written in intricate cipher. Step-by-step, amazed cryptographers deciphered the concealed history of Elizabethan England and with it the true identity of Francis Bacon as the rightful heir to the English throne, the *fils naturel* of Queen Elizabeth and Lord Leicester. Francis was given over at birth to Sir Nicholas and his Puritan wife Lady Anne, who was present at the royal birth and, it is believed, pleaded for the life of the infant. Elizabeth, the daughter born to Anne Boleyn and Henry VIII, inherited her father's tyrannical nature. Having been rejected as a child, she constantly feared that her subjects privately sought a king in her stead and was always careful, therefore, to maintain absolute dominion over her court, her advisors, even her son. Although later historical documents hint at a secret marriage, such a remark heard by the queen herself often resulted in imprisonment or death. Thus the true account of her reign is revealed perhaps solely in the coded writings of Francis Bacon. His childhood with Nicholas and good Lady Anne was spent happily and at age twelve he entered Cambridge, mysteriously funded by the queen herself. At age fifteen, however, Bacon unexpectedly left the university on a secret mission for the Crown. At this point it is believed that Francis discovered his true identity and was therefore hastily sent abroad by the queen for the purpose of setting him at a comfortable distance to her throne. Nevertheless, he was entrusted with the vital mission of studying the cipher-codes of Europe and developing new formulas for the protection of confidential information in England. Lord Bacon later recorded his understanding of literary science in *De Augmentis Scientiarum,* the *Advancement of Learning,* from which early cryptographers derived the formula for his work. Bacon's literal cipher has likewise revealed the inner teachings of the Brotherhood, the secrets of mysticism written in the "sacred language" of the hidden cipher understood only by advanced initiates, including those in the early Masonic Order. While in France, Bacon studied secret diplomacy and worked with an underground literary society called the Pleiades whose goal was the refinement of the French language. After three years, he returned to Britain with the intent of founding similar societies for the perfection of the English language and with the hope of diplomatically winning his rightful place as heir to the throne. Following his study of law at Grey's Inn, Bacon

served as a barrister in Parliament and wrote "A Letter of
Advice" to Queen Elizabeth in which he reveals remarkable political judgment. But Elizabeth denied Bacon even mere recognition, slighting him before her court and deliberately refus-
ing him positions of authority. Therefore, Bacon resolved, "I
will take all of learning to be my province." To historians ignorant of the relationship of Bacon and the queen, her disparaging
treatment of him was unexplainable and prompted much of the
literary investigation. Upon the passing of Queen Elizabeth in
1603, however, King James I appointed Francis Bacon to succeeding high positions, eventually awarding him the Lord Chancellor-
ship and the titles Baron Verulam and Viscount St. Albans. His
fame increased by the publication in 1620 of his most celebrated
work *Novum Organum*, the "New Instrument," in which Bacon
presents a series of syllogisms representing his inductive method and establishing his famous classification of the "Idols" of
the human mind which prohibit the understanding of divine
truth. He defines the "Idols of the Tribe" as inherent limitations
of the mortal mind, "Idols of the Cave" caused by human preju-
dice, "Idols of the Market Place" arising from man's inexact-
ness in the use of language, and "Idols of the Theatre" perpetu-
ated in various fallacious systems of thought. Bacon's numerous
philosophical works, including *Novum Organum* and *De Augmentis Scientiarum*, form integral parts of a grand comprehensive scheme for the restoration of wisdom—the *Instauratio
Magna*, the "Great Plan." Francis Bacon translated the King
James version of the Bible. His *Essays* are what he called
"dispersed meditations" on friendship, love, wealth, studies,
honor, and other fundamental graces of life. These witty, pithy
statements have become popular mottos and perhaps the most
familiar of his writings. *De Sapientia Veterum* is a brilliant
allegorical interpretation and scientific explanation of the
inner truths found in Greek mythology. Bacon founded a secret literary society in England known as the Helmet Bearers.
(Their patroness Pallas Athena was often pictured wearing a
helmet and full armor in her defense of truth. The traditions
of ancient Greece depict her standing atop her majestic temple, holding a golden spear which, when glinted upon by the
dawning sun, appeared to tremble. She is therefore known as
the "shaker of the spear" and thus the Shakespearean plays
truly received their name.) Francis Bacon sponsored the early
society of the Rosy Cross, the Rosicrucian Order, and was in-
strumental in founding the Masonic Order. From his famous
New Atlantis, the Masons derive their heritage of the House of
Solomon and the Masonic tradition of America as the Promised
Land where golden-age culture and science will rise again.
Later in 1620, fierce jealousy of Bacon's literary and political

success by members of Parliament resulted in his accusation of graft, later proven unjust. Bacon resigned his positions and spent the remaining years of his recorded life completing other valuable works, including the *History of Henry the VII* and his famous *Apophthegms.* In 1626, he feigned a "philosophic death" and attended his own funeral in disguise. Thereafter, he moved to the Rakoczy Mansion, located in the Carpathian foothills of Transylvania where Saint Germain, prior to the sinking of Atlantis, transported the flame of freedom from the Temple of Purification. There he took his final initiations under the Great Divine Director, his guru. Saint Germain won his ascension on May 1, 1684, after having made, as he once commented, "two million right decisions" during hundreds of thousands of years of service on behalf of earth and her evolutions.

SAINT GERMAIN as Prince Rakoczy, the Comte de Saint Germain, the "Wonderman of Europe." Upon his ascension from the Rakoczy Mansion in 1684, Ascended Master Saint Germain entered the Great Silence (nirvana) where his beloved twin flame Portia, the Goddess of Justice—whose name he had inscribed in *The Merchant of Venice*—had long been waiting his return. Not long thereafter, the beloved Sanctus Germanus was given the dispensation by the Lords of Karma to function in the world of form as an ascended being having the appearance of an unascended being. During this period, historians who have studied the life of the Wonderman of Europe have speculated that he was Prince Rakoczy, of the royal house of Hungary, which for centuries fought to maintain independence and religious liberty in Transylvania against the fierce attack of the Turks and the relentless invasion of the Hapsburg's powerful Austrian army. Ferencz Rákóczi I (1645-1676) was killed in the bitter struggles of the Hungarian Patriot Movement and upon his death the widowed princess, his children, and all their properties were seized by the Austrian emperor. In March, 1688, arrangements were made for his son Ferencz II (Francis Leopold Rakoczy) to be brought up in the Court of Vienna. When he came of age, the young prince regained his estate, although with considerable regulations and limitations. After his marriage in 1694, Ferencz II began to incite anew the fight for freedom in the small but exceedingly powerful and wealthy province of Transylvania. With the military assistance of Louis XIV of France, he waged several successful campaigns against both the Austrians and the Turks. In 1697, however, France withdrew her support and Ferencz II was forced to leave his wife and sons and take refuge in Poland. He then traveled to both France and Turkey in an attempt to regain support for his revolutionary cause, but to no avail. Transylvania was again captured by the Hapsburg government and two of the Rakoczy sons were forced to abandon their name and take the Austrian catholic names St. Karl and St. Elizabeth. In one account concerning the mysterious "third son," Prince Karl of Hesse writes: " [Saint Germain] told me that...he was the son of Prince Ragoczy of Transylvania by his first wife, Tékéli. He was placed, when quite young, under the care of the last Duc de Medici (Gian Gastone)....When M. de St. Germain learned that his two brothers, sons of the Princess of Hesse-Wahnfried (Rheihfels), had become subject to the Emperor Charles VI and had received the titles and names St. Karl and St. Elizabeth, he said to himself: 'Very well, I will call myself Sanctus Germano, the Holy Brother [Latin Sanctus Germanus].'" Saint Germain has neither confirmed nor denied whether, as the Wonderman of Europe, he chose to actually embody in the family of Ferencz II or whether he simply materialized a body and made it appear that he had descended through the royal house of Hungary, using the name and identity as a convenient disguise. It is not important to know which alternative he chose but to know that, as an ascended master, he could have chosen either one or both, since an ascended master may occupy any number of 'bodies', i.e., forcefields, simultaneously in order to accomplish his mission on earth. Note that during the period of his seeming ubiquitousness in Europe, he played an energetic and principal role in the American Revolution. The question may well be asked, where has the Master's presence not been felt in the universal movement for freedom which has taken place in the centuries leading up to the Aquarian dispensation? Throughout the courts of eighteenth century Europe, he was known as the Comte de Saint Germain. He appeared, disappeared, and reappeared in and out of royal circles with his outstanding quality of realism in an age that was closing in upon itself by the weight of its own hypocrisy. Voltaire aptly described him in a letter to Frederick II of Prussia as "a man who never dies and who knows everything." The archives of France contain evidence that English, Dutch, and Prussian statesmen of his time regarded the Count as an authority in many fields. He was hated by some while loved and held in awe by others. As one of his friends said, "He was, perhaps, one of the greatest philosophers who ever lived....His heart was concerned only with the happiness of others." The master alchemist spoke French, German, English, Italian, Spanish, Portuguese, and Russian so fluently that he was accepted as a native wherever he went. According to a contemporary account, "the learned and the oriental scholars have proved the knowledge of the Count St. Germain. The former found him more apt in the languages of Homer and Virgil than themselves; with the latter he spoke Sanscrit, Chinese, Arabic in such a manner as to show them that he had made some lengthy stay in Asia." The Comte de Saint Germain composed, improvised, accompanied on piano without music "not only every song but also the most difficult *concerti,* played on various instruments," and played the violin "like an orchestra." His compositions remain today in the British Museum and the library of the castle of Raudnitz in Bohemia. He painted in oils with colors of gemlike brilliance, a "secret" which he himself discovered. It is said that from 1737 to 1742, Saint Germain was at the Court of the Shah of Persia, there exhibiting his extraordinary knowledge of precipitating and perfecting precious stones, particularly diamonds. According to the memoirs of Madame du Hausset, Saint Germain once removed a flaw from a large diamond which belonged to King Louis XV. In his alchemical laboratory at the Royal Chateau at Chambord, Saint Germain was attended by a group of learned and noble students. The Count is described by Graf Cobenzl in a letter dated 1763: "Possessing great wealth, he lives in the greatest simplicity; he knows everything, and shows an uprightness, a goodness of soul, worthy of admiration. Among a number of his accomplishments, he made, under my own eyes, some experiments, of which the most important were the transmutation of iron into a metal as beautiful as gold." The Comte de Saint Germain thoroughly understood the use of herbs and plants and discovered medicines and elixirs to prolong life and maintain health. Many of his demonstrations of mastery are described in the diaries of Mme. d' Adhemar, who knew him for at least half a century. She records Saint Germain's visits to herself and to the courts of Louis XV and Louis XVI, noting in his glowing face the appearance of a man in his early forties throughout the period. She mentions a personal conversation with the Count in 1789 in which he appeared "with the same countenance as in 1760." In the same conversation he predicted the Revolution of 1789, the fall of the House of Bourbon, and the course of modern French history. Introducing the science of modern diplomacy, he carried out many secret diplomatic missions for the king to the courts of Europe. Had Saint Germain's counsel been heeded by Louis XVI, it would have prevented the French Revolution. Later Saint Germain sought to establish a United States of Europe through Napoleon (1799-1815), who failed his initiation and misused the master's power to his own demise. For more information, see *The Count of Saint-Germain* by Isabel Cooper-Oakley available from The Summit Lighthouse, paperback, $2.50 postpaid. Speaking of his efforts in the 18th century, Saint Germain said, "Having failed in securing the attention of the Court of France and others of the crowned heads of Europe, I turned myself to the perfectionment of mankind at large, and I recognized that there were many who, hungering and thirsting after

righteousness, would indeed be filled with the concept of a perfect union which would inspire them to take dominion over the
New World and create a union among the sovereign states. Thus
the United States was born as a child of my heart and the American Revolution was the means of bringing freedom in all of its
glory into manifestation from the East unto the West."

**SAINT GERMAIN, Ascended Master of the Aquarian Age,
Sponsor of the United States of America.** In 1775, a committee
appointed by the Continental Congress (including Franklin,
Lynch, and Harrison) met with Gen. Washington and a "mysterious old professor" in Cambridge, Mass. to recommend a
plan for the American flag. In this disguise, Saint Germain revealed his design for a flag with a variable field of stars—a
prophecy of the continual unfoldment of the vast destiny of the
new nation. Saint Germain broke the deadlock at Independence
Hall with his "Sign that document!" shouted from the balcony.
It was 5:00 p.m., July 4, 1776. The delegates signed the Declara-
tion of Independence, and when they looked up to thank him, the
"mysterious stranger" had come and gone. Saint Germain stood
by George Washington throughout the Revolution and during the
long winter at Valley Forge. He inspired and directed the writing
of the Constitution and anointed George Washington first presi-
dent of the United States. In the early 1930s, Saint Germain contacted his "general in the field," the reembodied George Washington, Guy W. Ballard, whom he trained as a messenger for hierarchy and through whom he released the dispensation of the violet-
flame energy of the Holy Spirit. Soon after, El Morya undertook
the training of the Messengers Mark and Elizabeth Prophet, who
were anointed by Saint Germain and called by the Darjeeling
Council to establish The Summit Lighthouse as the open door for
the release of the teachings of the ascended masters and the
establishment of the Community of the Holy Spirit in the Aquarian age. Following the ascension of Mark Prophet in 1973,
Elizabeth Clare Prophet remains the embodied messenger for
Saint Germain and the ascended masters. Today Saint Germain
uses Summit University, sponsored by Jesus Christ and Gau-
tama Buddha, to present his teachings on alchemy. With the
World Teachers Jesus and Kuthumi, he is working with children
preschool through twelfth grade at Montessori International.
Saint Germain sponsored the founding of the Boy and Girl
Scouts through Lord Baden-Powell and Juliette Gordon Low.
Within Church Universal and Triumphant, Saint Germain rep-
resents the Father, Mary, the Mother, and Jesus, the Christ, the
Son. In lectures and seminars throughout America and abroad,
Elizabeth Clare Prophet initiates chelas of Saint Germain on the
path of soul liberation. It is the prayer of devotees of the Great

Alchemist that many chelas will come forth so that Saint Germain will once again receive the dispensation from the Lords of Karma to step through the veil as he did as the Wonderman of Europe. To this end, Keepers of the Flame dedicate their energies in the giving of dynamic decrees to the violet flame in the science of the spoken Word. For them, Saturday night is world service to Saint Germain for personal and planetary freedom for earth's evolutions. Until Saint Germain and other members of the Great White Brotherhood step physically through the veil, they will continue to "step through" their embodied messengers, delivering their dictations, transferring their energy from Spirit to Matter, and initiating souls on the path of the ascension.

Notes

Chapter I

1. Rev. 3:15-16.
2. Pss. 136.
3. Pss. 2:7; Acts 13:33; Heb. 1:5; 5:5.
4. Rom. 4; James 2:23.
5. Zech. 4:6.
6. John 14:12.
7. Acts 10:15.
8. Matt. 21:42.
9. Heb. 9:23.

Chapter II

1. Gen. 1:26.
2. Luke 21:19.
3. Eph. 5:26.

Chapter III

1. Destiny: *Deity estab-lished in you.*
2. Prov. 22:6.
3. The establishment of a fountain of cosmic light over the city of Los Angeles was announced by the Great Silent Watcher at the Class of the Angels on September 21, 1963 "for a period of one hundred years or as long as the Great Law will permit." This tripartite etheric fountain extends thirty miles in diameter. The outer ring is composed of a blue fountain of cosmic faith rising one mile high above the city; the next ring, one mile within the blue, is a golden fountain of cosmic illumination twenty-eight miles wide and one mile and a half high; and in the center there is a pink fountain of cosmic love twenty-six miles across and two miles high. After the announcement, mighty Victory said, "We are laying the foundation stone here tonight for mankind's cosmic victory." Such a fountain of cosmic light may be established by the hierarchy with the assistance of the angel devas and builders of form wherever students faithfully invoke and visualize the fountain described.

4. Pss. 23:1.
5. Matt. 23:24.
6. 1 Cor. 15:54.

Chapter IV

1. Gen. 2:9.
2. Heb. 13:8.
3. Matt. 6:33.
4. Alfred Lord Tennyson, "Sir Galahad," stanza 1.

Chapter V

1. Gen. 3:22-23.
2. Heb. 12:1.

Chapter VI

1. Matt. 4:3.
2. *Webster's Seventh New Collegiate Dictionary* defines noblesse oblige (literally, nobility obligates) as "the obligation of honorable, generous, and responsible behavior associated with high rank or birth"; that is, the sons of God, because of their high birth and heritage, are obliged to invoke the will of God and to practice the science of alchemy selflessly on behalf of all mankind.
3. See the Great Divine Director, *The Mechanization Concept* (Washington, D.C.: The Summit Lighthouse, 1965).
4. John 10:10.
5. 1 Cor. 15:51-52.

Chapter VII

1. Matt. 5:1.
2. Gen. 30:25-43.
3. Matt. 6:1.
4. Heb. 13:2.
5. 2 Cor. 3:18.
6. Matt. 21:1-7.
7. Mark 11:1-7.

Chapter VIII

1. Rev. 12:1.
2. Rev. 4:6; 15:2.
3. 1 Cor. 14:8.
4. Matt. 3:17.
5. Matt. 16:26.
6. Matt. 10:16.
7. Isa. 11:9.
8. Acts 1:9, 11.
9. Matt. 24:40.
10. 2 Cor. 12:2.
11. Exod. 13:21.

Chapter IX

1. Saint Germain is using the term in its broad interpretation, "any pleasure in being abused or dominated" *(Webster's Seventh New Collegiate Dictionary,* s.v. "masochism").
2. Matt. 6:28-29.
3. 1 Cor. 9:26.

Chapter X

1. Luke 18:17.
2. Gen. 2:17.
3. Matt. 23:37.

4. 1 Cor. 2:9.
5. Matt. 28:18.
6. Gen. 3:24.
7. 1 Cor. 15:47-50.
8. Matt. 5:13.
9. Saint Germain uses the term "senile" here to mean approaching the end of an age.
10. Innocence: inner sense.

Chapter XI

1. John 3:17.
2. John 5:17.
3. Matt. 5:48.
4. Mark 10:32-34.
5. Luke 1:52.

6. Mater: The Mother or feminine aspect of creation which throughout the universe manifests as Matter. It is through this Mother aspect that the Spirit of God, the Father, evolves the consciousness of the Christ.

Chapter XII

1. Matt. 24:22.
2. Mark 16:17.
3. Ideation: I AM Deity in action.
4. Isa. 40:6-8.
5. Matt. 14:15-21.
6. John 6:19.

Mark L. Prophet

Mark L. Prophet
Now the Ascended Master Lanello

The Ascended Master Lanello, twentieth-century prophet, messenger of the Great White Brotherhood.

Thousands of years ago, the bodhisattva Sanat Kumara came from Venus to keep the flame of life on Earth. Lanello and his twin flame and other light evolutions of the planets of this solar system were among the sons and daughters of God who accompanied the Ancient of Days. The history of Lanello's mission is the story of a soul seized with a passion that is the love of God.

On Atlantis, he was a priest of the sacred fire and master of invocation in the Temple of the Logos. He lived as Lot, "Abram's brother's son," in the twentieth century B.C.—the man of God in the wretched cities of the plain, Sodom and Gomorrah. Thirty-three hundred years ago, as the Egyptian Pharaoh Ikhnaton, he overthrew the tradition of idolatry, challenged the false priesthood, and established a monotheism based on the worship of Aton, God of the Sun. During his reign, Egypt enjoyed a golden age of art, poetry, and music. As Aesop, he was a Greek slave in the sixth century B.C. who won his freedom as a master of didactic stories and fables, though he was murdered by the townspeople he sought to serve.

Then as Mark the Evangelist, he wrote the account of the works of Jesus—the Gospel of Deeds—as confided to him by Peter the Apostle. His mother was one of the most devoted of the women disciples, and Mark remembered when, as a boy, Jesus celebrated the Last Supper in the upper room. He was raised an Essene and, being well educated, was chosen Peter's chief disciple and secretary and was taken to Antioch to assist Paul. He became an exponent of the deeper mysteries of Christianity and founded the Church at Alexandria, where he was later martyred.

As Origen of Alexandria, he returned in the second century to the city he founded as St. Mark and became known as one of the most distinguished theologians of the early Church, setting forth the true teachings of Jesus Christ on reincarnation and the heavenly hierarchy. At the age of eighteen, he was appointed head of the Catechetical School— the first institution where Christians could be instructed in both the Greek sciences and the doctrines of Holy Scripture. He lived as an ascetic, working day and night with the crowds, lecturing and giving personal consultation. He made a thorough study of Plato, Pythagoras, and the Stoics and learned Hebrew in order to properly interpret Scripture. But his deep understanding seemed to shallow, worldly minds fantastic and heretical.

Banished from Egypt, Origen nevertheless became an honored teacher in Palestine at Caesarea where he established a school famous throughout the East. He was imprisoned during the persecution of Decius, tortured, and later died. Origen left behind a massive body of writings, numbering close to one thousand titles. His books were widely used for more than a century, but not without harsh criticism. In the fifth century, Rufinus of Aquieleia translated and made significant alterations in Origen's work, and Jerome condemned his teaching as heresy. In the sixth century, a list of fifteen anathemata were drawn up by Emperor Justinius in the Fifth Ecumenical

Council, followed by the physical destruction of his writings of which few remain today.

In the days of Arthur the King, the soul of Lanello came from France as Launcelot du Lac. According to legend, the infant Launcelot was laid down beside a lake and the Lady of the Lake carried him off to her kingdom of 10,000 maidens where no man was allowed. Here he matured in great honor and purity and thus was known as Launcelot du Lac (Launcelot of the Lake). He became Arthur's closest friend, their soul-relationship that of guru and chela, and the champion of Queen Guenevere, his twin flame. The jealousy, intrigue, and witchcraft of Modred and Morgana La Fey challenged the deep mutual love of the 'trinity' of Camelot driving wedges of distrust between king and queen, knight champion, and the other knights of the Round Table, ending in the death of Arthur and most of the knights and the seclusion of Guenevere and Launcelot in respective roles as renunciates of the Church.

As Clovis, he was the first of the Louis kings and established the French monarchy in the sixth century. He married his twin flame, then the Burgundian princess Clothilde, a Christian, and was baptized after successfully challenging her God to give him victory in battle. He became a devoted representative of the Church, and Clovis and Clothilde became patron saints of France as the founders of the nation and patron and patroness of the poor.

Then as Saladin, the great Moslem leader of the twelfth century, he conquered and united all of the Mohammedan world. Although a powerful general, Saladin is remembered for his generosity, gentleness, honesty, and justice to both Arabs and Christians alike.

As Saint Bonaventure, Seraphic Doctor of the Church, "prince of the mystics," he was the child healed by Saint Francis of Assisi who declared "O buona ventura!"—O good fortune! and thus the boy received his name. Together with Thomas Aquinas, a Dominican, Bonaventure, a Franciscan, played an important role in defending the mendicant orders in the thirteenth century.

He was Louis XIV, King of France from 1643 to 1715 (the longest recorded reign in European history), known as "le Roi Soleil," the Sun King. He sought to outpicture his soul-memory of the culture of Venus in the magnificent palace and gardens of Versailles.

As Longfellow, he became the most popular of American poets of the nineteenth century. He was an excellent teacher, first at Bowdoin and later presiding over the modern language program at Harvard for eighteen years. Longing for literary freedom, however, he left his post and began writing the poetry which captured the spirit and heart of America and the abiding flame of his guru, El Morya. It was his own soul of which Longfellow wrote in the narrative poem of the legendary Iroquois chief "Hiawatha."

As the twentieth-century master, Mark L. Prophet, he was born in Chippewa Falls, Wisconsin, in 1918, the only child of Thomas and Mabel Prophet. His father passed on when he was nine, and he and his mother endured the hardships of the depression years. When a boy of about eighteen, while working on the Sioux Line Railroad, he was contacted by Ascended Master El Morya, calling him to his mission. During World War II, he served in the U.S. Air Force and his training under the master continued. In 1958, El Morya directed him to found The Summit Lighthouse in the nation's capital. Mark himself typed the first dictations given by the ascended masters, called "Ashram Notes." He was joined by his twin flame, Elizabeth, in 1961, and together they fulfilled the prophecy of Jesus set forth by John the Revelator of holding the office of the "Two Witnesses" and the "Other Two" in this age. (See Rev. 11:3 and Dan. 12:5.) Together, Mark and Elizabeth Prophet held conferences throughout the world and founded the ascended masters' university in Santa Barbara in 1971.

On February 26, 1973, Mark passed on and his soul ascended to the plane of the I AM Presence to carry on his work with the ascended masters and to make contact with their unascended chelas. As the Ascended Master Lanello, he continues to direct the activities of The Summit Lighthouse, the "Ever-Present Guru" who has said: "Ours must be a message of infinite love and we must demonstrate that love to the world."

Elizabeth Clare Prophet is known today to the devotees of the teachings of the ascended masters as 'Mother' because of her devotion to the flame of God as Mother, and also as 'Guru Ma' in recognition of the mantle bestowed upon her by the gurus ascended and unascended of the Himalayas. She instructs and initiates students of cosmic law during twelve-week retreats sponsored by Jesus Christ and Gautama Buddha at Summit University. She also lectures and holds retreats throughout the world while continuing the important work of recording the teachings of the Great White Brotherhood and directing the multifaceted activities of Church Universal and Triumphant.

The lake—a jewel in the midst of the verdant, expansive acreage of Camelot—reflects the inner Self of the soul. Here people from all over the world come for twelve-week quarters at Summit University, two-week summer retreats, and weekend healing retreats to find God, soul freedom, a new way of life, and wholeness in the teachings of the ascended masters.

Glossary

Words set in *italics* are defined elsewhere in the Glossary

Adept. A true adept is an initiate of the *Great White Brotherhood* of a high degree of attainment; one undergoing advanced initiations of the *sacred fire* on the path of the *ascension*.

Akashic records. All that transpires in *Matter* is recorded in akasha—*"etheric"* energy vibrating at a certain frequency so as to absorb, or record, all of the impressions of life. These records can be read by those whose *soul* faculties are developed.

Alpha and Omega. Ascended *twin flames* who hold the awareness of God in the *Great Central Sun* in the white-fire core of our *cosmos*. They are mentioned in the Book of Revelation as the beginning and the ending (Rev. 1:8). Thus the Father is the origin and the Mother is the fulfillment of the cycles of God's consciousness throughout the creation. *See also* Mother.

Angel. An 'angle' of God's consciousness; an aspect of his Self-awareness; an individualization of the creative fires of the *cosmos*. The angelic hosts are an evolution of beings set apart from the evolutions of mankind by their flaming selfhood and by their purity of devotion to the Godhead and to the God-free beings they serve. Their function is to concentrate, intensify, and amplify the energies of God on behalf of the entire creation. They minister to the needs of mankind by intensifying feelings of hope, faith, and charity, honor and integrity, truth and freedom, mercy and justice, and every aspect of the crystal clarity of the mind of God.

Angels are electrons revolving around the Sun Presence that is God—electrons who have elected to expand his consciousness in every plane of being. They are rods and cones of concentrated energy that can be diverted into action by the Christed ones wherever and whenever there is a need. There are angels of healing, protection, love, comfort and compassion, angels attending the cycles of life and death, angels who wield the flaming sword of truth to cleave asunder the real from the unreal. There are types and orders of angels who perform specific services in the cosmic *hierarchy.*

The fallen angels are those who followed *Lucifer* in the Great Rebellion and whose consciousness therefore "fell" to lower levels of awareness as they were by law "cast out into the earth" (Rev. 12:9) where they continue to amplify the luciferian rebellion. They are known as the fallen ones, the sons of Belial, the Luciferians.

Angel deva. *See* Deva.

Archangel. An *angel* who has passed certain advanced initiations qualifying him to preside over lesser angels and bands of angels. Each of the *seven rays* has an archangel who, with his divine complement, an *archeia,* presides over the angels serving on that *ray.* The archangels and archeiai of the rays are as follows: First ray, *Archangel Michael* and Faith; second ray,

Archangel Jophiel and Christine; third ray, Archangel Chamuel and Charity; fourth ray, Archangel Gabriel and Hope; fifth ray, Archangel Raphael and Mary; sixth ray, Archangel Uriel and Aurora; seventh ray, *Archangel Zadkiel* and Holy Amethyst.

Archangel Michael. *Archangel* of the First *Ray,* who stands as the defender of the *Christ consciousness* in all mankind. He is the protagonist of the *Divine Mother;* he cast the dragon and his *angels* out of heaven into the earth (Rev. 12: 7-9). Michael, Prince of the Archangels (Dan. 10:13), is also referred to as Saint Michael, the Defender of the Faith. His divine complement is the *archeia* Faith. Their *retreat* is located on the *etheric plane* in the Canadian Rockies at Lake Louise, Banff, Alberta.

Archangel Zadkiel. *Archangel* of the Seventh *Ray,* who focuses the consciousness of God-freedom on behalf of souls evolving in the planes of *Matter.* Together with his *twin flame,* the *archeia* Holy Amethyst, Lord Zadkiel teaches mankind the science of alchemy, the ritual of invocation, and prepares them for the priesthood in the order of Melchizedek. His *retreat* is the Temple of Purification located on the *etheric plane* over the island of Cuba.

Archeia (*pl.* **archeiai**). Feminine complement and *twin flame* of an *archangel.*

Ascended being. *See* Ascended master.

Ascended master. One who has mastered time and space and in the process gained the mastery of the self, balanced at least 51 percent of his *karma,* fulfilled his *divine plan,* and ascended into the *Presence* of the I AM THAT I AM; one who inhabits the planes of *Spirit,* or heaven.

Ascension. The ritual whereby the *soul* reunites with the *Spirit,* the *I AM Presence.* The ascension is the final initiation of the soul after its sojourn in time and space. It is the reward of the righteous that is the gift of God after the final judgment in which every man is judged according to his works (Rev. 20:12). The ascension was demonstrated publicly by Elijah, who ascended "in a chariot of fire" (2 Kings 2:11), and by *Jesus,* who ascended from Bethany's hill (Luke 24:50-51). It is the goal of life for the *sons and daughters of God.*

Astral. (1) *adj.* Having or carrying the characteristics of the *astral plane.* (2) *n.* A frequency of time and space beyond the physical yet below the mental, corresponding with the *emotional body* of man and the collective subconscious of the race. The term is also used in a negative context to refer to that which is impure or "psychic." *See also* Psychic.

Astral body. *See* Emotional body.

Astral plane. The plane on which the emotions of mankind register collectively. This plane is intended to be used for the amplification of the pure feelings of God; instead it has been polluted with the impure thoughts and feelings of mankind.

Atlantis. The continent which existed where the Atlantic Ocean now is and which sank in cataclysm. According to James Churchward, this occurred more than 11,600 years ago *(The*

Lost Continent of Mu [New York: Ives Washburn, 1931], p. 264).

Aura. The forcefield of energy surrounding the *soul* and the *four lower bodies* on which the impressions, thoughts, feelings, words, and actions of the individual are registered. It has been referred to as the L-field, which some scientists say controls the manifestation of the *physical body*.

Avatar. (<Skt *avatāra* descent, from *avatarati* he descends, from *ava-* away + *tarati* he crosses over) The incarnation of the *Word;* the descent or crossing-over of the universal *Christ* from the plane of *Spirit* to the plane of *Matter*. The avatar of an age is the Christed one who out-pictures in consciousness and in the *four lower bodies* the archetypal pattern of the Father-Mother God as an example for the evolution of *souls* in a two-thousand-year cycle. The principal avatars of an age are two in number—the masculine and feminine prototypes who show forth the path of initiation designated by the solar hierarchies responsible for the two-thousand-year dispensation. According to mankind's *karma* and the requirements of the Logos, the *Manus* may designate numerous avatars to go forth as teachers and wayshowers in a given epoch.

Ballard, Guy W. *Messenger* for the *Great White Brotherhood* from the late 1920s to the year 1939, when he made his *ascension* on December 31. Now the *ascended master* Godfre, also known as God Obedience. He was embodied as Richard the Lionhearted and as George Washington. In his final embodiment, with his wife and *twin flame,* Edna Ballard, he founded the I AM movement under the direction of the ascended master *Saint Germain.* His pen name was Godfre Ray King. His most important works are *Unveiled Mysteries, The Magic Presence,* and *The "I AM" Discourses.*

Bodies of man. The four lower bodies are four sheaths consisting of four distinct frequencies which surround the *soul*—the physical, emotional, mental, and *etheric.* They are the modes of the soul in its journey through time and space. The three higher bodies are the *Christ Self,* the *I AM Presence,* and the *causal body. See also* Chart of Your Divine Self, Etheric body, Mental body, Emotional body, and Physical body.

Brotherhood. *See* Great White Brotherhood.

Buddha. Taken from the Sanskrit root *budh,* meaning to wake up and to know. Buddha means "the enlightened one." It denotes an office in *hierarchy* that is attained by passing certain initiations of the *sacred fire,* including those of the *seven rays* of the *Holy Spirit* and of the five secret *rays,* the raising of the feminine ray, and the "mastery of the seven in the seven multiplied by the power of the ten." (See chap. 10 of *Intermediate Studies of the Human Aura* by Djwal Kul, published by The Summit Lighthouse.) Gautama attained the enlightenment of the Buddha twenty-five centuries ago during his forty-nine-day meditation under the Bo tree; hence he is called Gautama, the Buddha. He holds the office of Lord of the World because he has the highest attainment of the evolutions of Terra and is excelled by none in his devotion to the *World Mother. Lord*

Maitreya, the Cosmic *Christ,* has also passed the initiations of the Buddha; and in the great history of the planet, there have been numerous Buddhas who have served the evolutions of mankind.

In the 1960s, nine unascended lifestreams who had passed the initiations of the Buddha volunteered to embody to assist the evolutions of Terra during the transition into the age of Aquarius. Their world service will be recognized when they have reached the age of the Christic and Buddhic example, age thirty-three to thirty-six.

Carnal mind. The *human ego,* the human will, and the human intellect; self-awareness without the *Christ;* the animal nature of man. "The carnal mind is enmity against God." (Rom. 8:7)

Causal Body. The body of First Cause; concentric spheres of *light* and consciousness surrounding the *I AM Presence* in the planes of *Spirit.* These concentric forcefields of electronic energy are available to the *soul* to work the works of God upon earth. The energies of the causal body may be drawn forth through invocation made to the I AM Presence in the name of the *Christ.* The causal body is the dwelling place of the Most High God to which *Jesus* referred when he said, "In my Father's house are many mansions" (John 14:2). The causal body is the mansion or the habitation of the Spirit to which the soul returns through the ritual of the *ascension.* The causal body as the star of each man's divine individuality was referred to by Paul when he said, "One star differeth from another star in glory" (1 Cor. 15:41). *See also* Chart of Your Divine Self.

Cave of Symbols. *Etheric* as well as physical *retreat* of the master *Saint Germain,* located in the Rockies in the environs of Wyoming. Here initiates of the seventh *ray* are taken in their finer bodies to prepare for the *ascension;* those who qualify receive directly from the master teachings in the sacred mysteries of Christhood. Saint Germain is the guardian of the records of ancient civilizations and of the achievements of science which will again be outpictured in the *golden age* of Aquarius.

Central sun. *See* Great Central Sun.

Chakra. Sanskrit for wheel, disc, circle. Term used to denote the centers of *light* anchored in the *etheric body* and governing the flow of energy to the four lower *bodies of man.* There are seven major chakras corresponding to the *seven rays,* five minor chakras corresponding to the five secret *rays,* and a total of 144 light centers in the body of man. The seven major chakras, their corresponding rays, Sanskrit names, and colors are as follows: First ray, throat, Vishuddha, blue; second ray, crown, Sahasrāra, yellow; third ray, heart, Anāhata, pink; fourth ray, base of the spine, Mūlādhāra, white; fifth ray, third eye, Ājnā, green; sixth ray, solar plexus, Manipūra, purple and gold; seventh ray, seat of the soul, Svādhishthāna, violet.

Chart of Your Divine Self. There are three figures represented in the chart, which we will refer to as the upper figure, the middle figure, and the lower figure. The upper figure is the *I AM Presence,* the I AM THAT I AM, God individualized for every son and daughter of the flame. The Divine Monad consists of the I AM Presence surrounded by the spheres (rings of color, of *light*) which comprise the *causal body*. This is the body of First Cause that contains within it man's "treasure laid up in heaven"—perfect works, perfect thoughts and feelings, perfect words—energies that have ascended from the plane of action in time and space as the result of man's correct exercise of *free will* and his correct qualification of the stream of life that issues forth from the heart of the Presence and descends to the level of the *Christ Self*.

The middle figure in the chart is the mediator between God and man, called the Christ Self, the *Real Self*, or the *Christ consciousness*. It has also been referred to as the Higher Mental Body. The Christ Self overshadows the lower self, which consists of the *soul* evolving through the four planes of *Matter* in the *four lower bodies* corresponding to the planes of earth, air, fire, and water; that is, the *etheric body*, the *mental body*, the *emotional body*, the *physical body*.

The three figures of the chart correspond to the Trinity of Father (the upper figure), Son (the middle figure), and *Holy Spirit* (the lower figure), which the evolving soul is intended to become and for whom the body is the temple. The lower figure is the nonpermanent aspect of being which is made permanent through the ritual of the *ascension*. The ascension is the process whereby the lower figure, having balanced his *karma* and fulfilled his *divine plan*, merges first with the Christ consciousness and then with the living Presence of the I AM THAT I AM. Once the ascension has taken place, the soul, the corruptible aspect of being, becomes the incorruptible one, a permanent atom in the body of God. The Chart of Your Divine Self is therefore a diagram of yourself—past, present, and future.

The lower figure represents mankind evolving in the planes of Matter. This is how you should visualize yourself standing in the *violet flame,* which you invoke in the name of the I AM Presence and in the name of the *Christ* in order to purify your four lower bodies in preparation for the ritual of the alchemical marriage—your soul's reunion with the *Spirit,* the I AM Presence. The lower figure is surrounded by a *tube of light,* which is projected from the heart of the I AM Presence in answer to your call. It is a field of fiery protection sustained in Spirit and in Matter for the sealing of the identity of the overcomer. The *threefold flame* within the heart is the spark of life projected from the I AM Presence through the Christ Self and anchored in the *etheric planes* in the heart *chakra* for the purpose of the soul's evolution in Matter. Also called the Christ flame, the threefold flame is the spark of man's divinity, his potential for Godhood.

The crystal cord is the stream of light that descends from the heart of the I AM Presence through the Christ Self, thence to the four lower bodies to sustain the soul's vehicles of expression in time and space. It is over this cord that the energy of the Presence flows, entering the being of man at the top of the head and providing the energy for the pulsation of the threefold flame and the physical heartbeat. When a round of the soul's incarnation in

YOUR DIVINE SELF

Chart of Your Divine Self

There are three figures represented in the chart, which we will refer to as the upper figure, the middle figure, and the lower figure. The upper figure is the I AM Presence, the I AM THAT I AM, God individualized for every son and daughter of God. The Divine Monad consists of the I AM Presence surrounded by the spheres (rings of color, of light) which comprise the causal body. This is the body of First Cause that contains within it man's "treasure laid up in heaven"—perfect works, perfect thoughts and feelings, perfect words—energies that have ascended from the plane of action in time and space as the result of man's correct exercise of free will and his correct qualification of the stream of life that issues forth from the heart of the Presence and descends to the level of the Christ Self.

The middle figure in the chart is the mediator between God and man, called the Christ Self, the Real Self, or the Christ consciousness. It has also been referred to as the Higher Mental Body or Higher Consciousness. The Christ Self overshadows the lower self, which consists of the soul evolving through the four planes of Matter in the four lower bodies corresponding to the planes of earth, air, fire, and water; that is, the etheric body, the mental body, the emotional body, the physical body.

The three figures of the chart correspond to the Trinity of Father (the upper figure), Son (the middle figure), and Holy Spirit. The lower figure is intended to become the temple for the Holy Spirit which is indicated in the enfolding violet-flame action of the sacred fire. The lower figure corresponds to you as a disciple on the Path. Your soul is the nonpermanent aspect of being which is made permanent through the ritual of the ascension. The ascension is the process whereby the soul, having balanced his karma and fulfilled his divine plan, merges first with the Christ consciousness and then with the living Presence of the I AM THAT I AM. Once the ascension has taken place, the soul, the corruptible aspect of being, becomes the incorruptible one, a permanent atom in the body of God. The Chart of Your Divine Self is therefore a diagram of yourself—past, present, and future.

The lower figure represents mankind evolving in the planes of Matter. This is how you should visualize yourself standing in the violet flame, which you invoke in the name of the I AM Presence and in the name of your Christ Self in order to purify your four lower bodies in preparation for the ritual of the alchemical marriage—your soul's union with the Lamb as the bride of Christ. The lower figure is surrounded by a tube of light, which is projected from the heart of the I AM Presence in answer to your call. It is a field of fiery protection sustained in Spirit and in Matter for the sealing of the individuality of the disciple. The threefold flame within the heart is the spark of life projected from the I AM Presence through the Christ Self and anchored in the etheric planes in the heart chakra for the purpose of the soul's evolution in Matter. Also called the Christ flame, the threefold flame is the spark of man's divinity, his potential for Godhood.

The crystal cord is the stream of light that descends from the heart of the I AM Presence through the Christ Self, thence to the four lower bodies to sustain the soul's vehicles of expression in time and space. It is over this cord that the energy of the Presence flows, entering the being of man at the top of the head and providing the energy for the pulsation of the threefold flame and the physical heartbeat. When a round of the soul's incarnation in Matter-form is complete, the I AM Presence withdraws the crystal cord, the threefold flame returns to the level of the Christ, and the energies of the four lower bodies return to their respective planes.

The dove of the Holy Spirit descending from the heart of the Father is shown just above the head of the Christ. When the individual man, as the lower figure, puts on and becomes the Christ consciousness as Jesus did, the descent of the Holy Spirit takes place and the words of the Father, the I AM Presence, are spoken, "This is my beloved Son in whom I AM well pleased" (Matt. 3:17).

A more detailed explanation of the Chart of Your Divine Self is given in the Keepers of the Flame Lessons and in *Climb the Highest Mountain* by Mark L. Prophet and Elizabeth Clare Prophet, published by Summit University Press.

Matter-form is complete, the I AM Presence withdraws the crystal cord, the threefold flame returns to the level of the Christ, and the energies of the four lower bodies return to their respective planes.

The dove of the Holy Spirit descending from the heart of the Father is shown just above the head of the Christ. When the individual man, as the lower figure, puts on and becomes the Christ consciousness as *Jesus* did, the descent of the Holy Spirit takes place and the words of the Father, the I AM Presence, are spoken, "This is my beloved Son in whom I AM well pleased" (Matt. 3:17).

A more detailed explanation of the Chart of Your Divine Self is given in the Keepers of the Flame Lessons and in *Climb the Highest Mountain* by Mark and Elizabeth Prophet, published by The Summit Lighthouse.

Chela. In India, a disciple of a religious teacher (<Hindi *celā* <Skt *ceṭa* slave). A term used generally to refer to a student of the *ascended masters* and their teachings. Specifically, a student of more than ordinary self-discipline and devotion initiated by an ascended master and serving the cause of the *Great White Brotherhood.*

Chohan. Tibetan for lord or master; a chief. Each of the *seven rays* has a chohan who focuses the *Christ consciousness* of the *ray.* The names of the chohans of the rays are as follows: First ray, *El Morya;* second ray, Lanto; third ray, Paul the Venetian; fourth ray, *Serapis Bey;* fifth ray, Hilarion; sixth ray, Nada; seventh ray, *Saint Germain.*

Christ. *Christos,* Grk., anointed one. The *Word,* the
Logos, the Second Person of the Trinity, the
only begotten Son of the Father full of grace and
truth, the *light* which lighteth every man that
cometh into the world (John 1:1-14). In the
Hindu Trinity of Brahma, Vishnu, and Shiva,
Christ corresponds to Vishnu, the Preserver.

The universal Christ is the mediator between
the planes of *Spirit* and the planes of *Matter.*
The universal Christ is the nexus of consciousness through which the energies of the
Father pass for the crystallization (*Christ-*
realization) of the God flame in the *Mother.*
This process is called materialization (*Mater-*
realization). The process whereby the energies
of the Mother pass through the nexus of the
Christ consciousness to the Father is called
spiritualization (*Spirit*-realization). Another
name for the process whereby energy returns
from Matter to Spirit is sublimation (sublime
action) or transmutation. The fusion of the
energies of the positive and negative polarity of
the Godhead in the creation takes place through
the universal Christ, the Logos "without whom
was not any thing made that was made." The
flow of light from the *Macrocosm* to the *microcosm,* from the Spirit (the *I AM Presence)*
to the *soul,* is fulfilled through the blessed
mediator, the Christ. This is the meaning of
the statement "I AM the open door which no
man can shut."

The term "Christ" also denotes an office in
hierarchy held by those who have attained self-
mastery on the *seven rays* and the seven
chakras of the *Holy Spirit.* Christ-mastery
includes the balancing of the *threefold flame*—

the aspects of love, wisdom, and power—for the harmonization of consciousness and the implementation of the mastery of the seven rays in the chakras and in the *four lower bodies.* At the hour designated for the *ascension,* the Christed one raises the spiral of the threefold flame from beneath the feet through the entire form for the transmutation of every atom and cell of his being, consciousness, and world. The saturation and acceleration of the four lower bodies and the soul by this light of the Christ flame takes place during the ascension.

The individual *Christ Self,* the personal Christ, is the initiator of every living soul. When the individual passes certain initiations on the path of Christhood, he earns the right to be called a Christed one and gains the title of *son or daughter of God.* Some who have earned that title in past ages have failed to manifest that attainment in subsequent incarnations. In this age the Logos requires them to bring forth their inner mastery and to perfect it. Therefore, to assist the sons and daughters of God in making their manifestation commensurate with their inner attainment, the masters of the *Great White Brotherhood* have released their teachings through their *messengers* in this century. Prior to the fulfillment of these initiations, the individual is referred to as a child of God.

Expanding the consciousness of the Christ, the Christed one then attains the realization of the Christ consciousness at a planetary level and is able to hold the balance of the Christ flame on behalf of the evolutions of a planet. When this is achieved, he assists members of hierarchy who serve in the office of the planetary Christ. *See also* Chart of Your Divine Self, Jesus.

Christ consciousness. The consciousness or awareness of the self as the *Christ;* the attainment of
a level of consciousness commensurate with
that which was realized by *Jesus* the Christ.
The Christ consciousness is the fulfillment
within the self of that mind which was in Christ
Jesus. It is the attainment of the balanced
awareness of *power, wisdom, and love*—of
Father, Son, and *Holy Spirit*—through the
balanced manifestation of the *threefold flame*
within the heart. *See also* Chart of Your Divine
Self.

Christ Self. The individualized focus of "the only
begotten of the Father full of grace and truth"
(John 1:14); the *universal Christ* individualized
as the true identity of the *soul;* the *Real Self* of
every man, woman, and child to which the soul
must rise. The Christ Self is the mediator
between a man and his God; it is a man's own
personal mentor, priest and prophet, master
and teacher. Total identification with the Christ
Self defines the Christed one, the Christed
being, or the *Christ consciousness. See also*
Chart of Your Divine Self.

City Foursquare. (See Rev. 21:10-26.) The New
Jerusalem; the mandala of the four planes of
Spirit and the four planes of *Matter* which John
saw as the "new heaven and the new earth"; the
four sides of the four planes of God's consciousness focused in Spirit and in Matter.
The twelve gates are gates of God's consciousness, the focuses of the twelve qualities of
the Godhead sustained by the twelve solar
hierarchies.

Unascended *souls* may invoke the mandala of
the City Foursquare for the fulfillment of the

God consciousness as above, so below. The City Foursquare is the blueprint of the solar identity of the *sons and daughters of God*. The *light* of the city is the Lord God Almighty, the *I AM Presence;* the Lamb is the *Christ Self;* the jewels are the 144 *chakras* and the frequencies of the light anchored in those chakras.

Color rays. The *light* emanations of the Godhead; e.g., the *seven rays* of the white light which emerge through the prism of the *Christ consciousness* are (1) blue, (2) yellow, (3) pink, (4) white, (5) green, (6) purple and gold, and (7) violet. There are also five "secret *rays*" which emerge from the white-fire core of being.

Cosmic being. An *ascended master* who has attained *cosmic consciousness* and ensouls the energies of many worlds and systems of worlds within this galaxy and beyond.

Cosmic consciousness. (1) God's awareness of himself in and as the *cosmos.* (2) Man's awareness of himself in and as God's cosmic self-awareness. The awareness of the self fulfilling the cycles of the cosmos; the awareness of the self as God in cosmic dimensions; the attainment of initiations leading to a cosmic awareness of selfhood.

Cosmic Egg. The spiritual-material universe, including a seemingly endless chain of galaxies, star systems, worlds known and unknown, whose center or white-fire core is called the *Great Central Sun.* The Cosmic Egg has both a spiritual and a material center. Although we discover the Cosmic Egg from the standpoint of our physical senses and perspective, all of the dimensions of *Spirit* can also be known and experienced within the Cosmic Egg. The Cosmic Egg represents the bounds of man's habitation in this cosmic cycle.

Cosmic law. That law which governs all manifestation throughout the *cosmos* in the planes of *Spirit* and *Matter*.

Cosmic Virgin. The *Divine Mother,* specifically in her awareness of the *cosmic consciousness* of wholeness.

Cosmos. The world or universe regarded as an orderly, harmonious system. The material cosmos consists of the entire manifestation in the planes of *Matter* of universes known and unknown. All that exists in time and space comprises the cosmos. There is also a spiritual cosmos, which includes the counterpart of the material cosmos and beyond.

Darjeeling Council. A council of the *Great White Brotherhood* headed by the *ascended master El Morya,* its chief. The Darjeeling Council trains *souls* in the laws of God and man and serves to implement the will of God and God-government upon earth. The council meets in the Temple of God's Will on the *etheric plane* over Darjeeling, India.

Decree. (1) *n.* (a) a foreordaining will, an edict or fiat, a foreordaining of events; (b) a prayer invoking the *light* of God for and on behalf of the evolutions of mankind in the name of the *Christ* and in the name of the *I AM Presence.* (2) *v.* (a) to decide, to declare, to command or enjoin; to determine or order; to ordain; (b) to invoke the light of God aloud by the power of the *spoken Word* in rhythm and in harmony.

The decree is the most powerful of all applications to the Godhead. It is the command of the *son or daughter of God* made in the name of the I AM Presence and the Christ for the will of the Almighty to come into manifestation as above, so below. It is the means whereby the kingdom of God becomes a reality here and now through the power of the spoken Word. It may be short or long and usually is marked by a formal preamble and a closing, or acceptance.

Deva. Sanskrit for radiant being. Member of an order of angelic beings who serve with the elemental forces of nature, assisting them to perform their various functions. *Angel* devas are the guardian spirits of the mountains and the forests. They also ensoul and hold the matrix for the *Christ consciousness* to be outpictured by the people of a particular locale—city, state, nation, or continent—or for a particular race, nationality, or ethnic group.

Diamond heart. A concentration of the fires of the will of God which coalesce as a diamond matrix in the hearts of those who are devoted to God's will. Hence, a term used to describe the heart of the *ascended masters, angel devas,* and *chelas* devoted to the will of God; often associated with Mary the Mother of *Jesus* and *El Morya.* The diamond heart of God possesses the quality of the diamond crystal, refracting the *light* of love throughout the creation and reflecting, magnifying, and projecting the virtues embodied by the *sons and daughters of God.*

Divine Ego. Awareness of true selfhood in and as the *Christ Self* or the *I AM Presence;* the Higher Self of man.

Divine Manchild. The Manchild born to the Woman
clothed with the Sun (Rev. 12) is the incarnation
of the *Christ* for the Aquarian age in the one and
the many *sons and daughters of God* whose
destiny it is to focus the *Christ consciousness* to
the evolutions of earth. Specifically, the term
"Manchild" refers to the child who has the
Holy Spirit from his mother's womb, e.g., John
the Baptist and *Jesus*.

Divine Mother. *See* Mother.

Divine plan. The plan of God for the individual *soul*
ordained in the beginning when the blueprint of
life was impressed upon the white-fire core of
the individual *I AM Presence*. The divine plan
determines the limits of the individual expression of *free will*. As the acorn is destined to be
the oak, so each individual soul is destined to
realize the fullness of the potential of the *Tree
of Life,* which is the I AM Presence and the
causal body. What that potential is, is known of
God and can be released to the outer consciousness through application to the individual
Christ Self, the I AM Presence, and the *Great
Divine Director.*

El Morya Khan. The *ascended master.* Lord
(Chohan) of the First *Ray* of God's Will, Chief of
the *Darjeeling Council* of the *Great White
Brotherhood,* founder of *The Summit Light-
house,* teacher and sponsor of the *messengers*
Mark and Elizabeth Prophet. El Morya was
embodied as the Irish poet Thomas Moore,
Akbar the Great, Sir Thomas More, Thomas à
Becket, and Melchior, one of the three wise
men.

Emotional body. One of the four lower *bodies of*

man; the body intended to be the vehicle of the desires and feelings of God made manifest in the being of man. Also called the *astral body,* the desire body, and the feeling body.

Etheric. Of or relating to that plane of *Matter* which vibrates at the highest frequency capable of being contained in Matter. The etheric frequency and its correspondent plane of consciousness is the repository of the fiery blueprint of the entire physical universe. Etheric energies provide the envelope or vehicle of the *soul* (etheric or memory body) and the plane of transition between the material and the spiritual universe.

Etheric body. One of the four lower *bodies of man;* called the envelope of the *soul,* holding the blueprint of the perfect image to be outpictured in the world of form. Also called the memory body.

Etheric plane. The highest plane in the dimension of *Matter;* a plane which is as concrete and real (and more so) as the physical plane but which is experienced through the senses of the *soul* in a dimension and a consciousness beyond physical awareness. The plane on which the records of mankind's entire evolution register individually and collectively.

Evil. Energy-*veil;* the veil of misqualified energy which man imposes upon *Matter* through his misuse of the *sacred fire.*

Four lower bodies. *See* Bodies of man, Physical body, Mental body, Emotional body, and Etheric body.

Free will. The freedom to create; the option to

choose the right- or the left-handed path, life or death, the positive or the negative spirals of consciousness. Having the gift of free will, the *soul* may choose to dwell in the plane of the relative, where good and *evil* are relative to one's perspective in time and space; or it may choose the plane of the Absolute, where good is real and evil is unreal and the soul beholds God as living Truth "face to face." Free will means that the individual may accept or reject the *divine plan,* the laws of God, and the opportunity to live in the consciousness of Love.

Free will carries with it a certain span of consciousness known as the "bounds of man's habitation." The soul, therefore, is not only confined to time and space during the period of its experimentation with free will, but also it is limited to a certain number of cycles which the soul interprets as its own "time and space." At the end of the cycles of opportunity, the use that the soul has made of the gift of free will determines its fate. The soul that has chosen to glorify the *Divine Ego* ascends into the Presence of the I AM THAT I AM; the soul that has chosen to glorify the *human ego* passes through the second death (Rev. 20:14), its identity permanently canceled and all of its energies returned to the *Great Central Sun* for repolarization.

God consciousness. The consciousness or awareness of the self as God; the awareness of the I AM THAT I AM, or the *I AM Presence;* the ability to maintain this conscious Self-awareness in God and to control the energies of this Self-awareness in the planes of *Matter* and *Spirit. See also* Cosmic consciousness.

Goddess of Justice. *See* Portia.

Goddess of Liberty. The ascended lady master who holds the *cosmic consciousness* of liberty for the earth. While embodied on *Atlantis,* she erected the Temple of the Sun where Manhattan Island now is. With the sinking of Atlantis the physical temple was destroyed, but the *etheric* counterpart remains on the *etheric plane* where she continues to focus the flame of liberty on the central altar surrounded by twelve shrines dedicated to the twelve hierarchies of the sun. The Goddess of Liberty is the Spokesman for the *Karmic Board* and represents the second *ray* on the board.

Godfre Ray King. *See* Ballard, Guy W.

God Presence. *See* I AM Presence.

God Self. *See* I AM Presence.

Golden age. A cycle of enlightenment, peace, and harmony wherein the *souls* of mankind merge in the *Christ* flame for the fulfillment of the *divine plan* "as above, so below" through "thy kingdom come on earth as it is in heaven."

Great Central Sun. The nucleus or white-fire core of the *Cosmic Egg.* (The God Star Sirius is the focus of the Great Central Sun in our sector of the galaxy.)

Great Divine Director. The *ascended master* whose attainment of *cosmic consciousness* enables him to ensoul the flame of divine direction throughout the universe. Founder of the House of Rakoczy, teacher of *Saint Germain,* sponsor and *Manu* of the *seventh root race,* he maintains a focus in the Cave of Light in India and in the House of Light in Transylvania, the

focus of freedom for eastern and western
Europe. The Great Divine Director represents
the first *ray* on the *Karmic Board*. He is also
known as the Master R.

Great White Brotherhood. The fraternity of saints,
sages, and *ascended masters* of all ages who,
coming from every nation, race, and religion,
have reunited with the *Spirit* of the living God
and who comprise the heavenly hosts. The term
"white" refers to the halo of white *light* that
surrounds their forms. The Great White
Brotherhood also includes in its ranks certain
unascended *chelas* of the ascended masters.

Hierarchy. The chain of individualized beings
fulfilling aspects of God's infinite selfhood.
Hierarchy is the means whereby God in the
Great Central Sun steps down the energies of
his consciousness, that succeeding evolutions in
time and space might come to know the wonder
of his love.

Holy Amethyst. *See* Archangel Zadkiel.

Holy Spirit. Third Person of the Trinity; the
omnipresence of God; the cloven tongues of fire
which focus the Father-Mother God, also called
the *sacred fire;* the energies of life that infuse a
cosmos. In the Hindu Trinity of Brahma,
Vishnu, and Shiva, the Holy Spirit corresponds
to Shiva, the Destroyer, because its all-
consuming energies, when invoked in the planes
of *Matter,* transmute the cause and effect of
man's miscreations. Prana is the essence of the
Holy Spirit which we take in through the
chakras to nourish the *four lower bodies.* The
Holy Spirit focuses the balance of the Father-
Mother God in the white-fire core of being.

The flame of the Holy Spirit is the Comforter which the Christed one promised would come when he took his leave of this plane (John 14:16; 16:7). Each time a *son or daughter of God* ascends into the Presence of the I AM THAT I AM, the Holy Spirit descends to fill the void.

The representative of the flame of the Holy Spirit to earth is the *ascended master* who occupies the office of *Maha Chohan*. The Holy Spirit is the Personal Impersonality of the Godhead and is represented on the west side of the *City Foursquare*. *See also* Chart of Your Divine Self.

Human consciousness. That consciousness which is aware of the self as human—limited, mortal, subject to error.

Human ego. The point of identity that embraces the *human consciousness* as selfhood.

Human monad. The entire forcefield of self which identifies itself as human. The lower figure in the *Chart of Your Divine Self;* the point of self-awareness out of which all mankind must evolve to the realization of the self as the *Christ*.

I AM Presence. The I AM THAT I AM (Exod. 3:13-15); the individualized Presence of God focused for each individual *soul*. The God-identity of the individual; the Divine Monad; the individual Source. The origin of the soul focused in the planes of *Spirit* just above the physical form; the personification of the God flame for the individual. *See also* Chart of Your Divine Self.

Jesus. The *ascended master* Jesus the Christ. The *avatar* of the Piscean age; the example of the *Christ consciousness* in that age; one who

realized the fullness of the *Christ Self* and was
therefore called Jesus, the *Christ*. He came to
reveal the individual Christ Self to all mankind
and to show the works of the Father (the *I AM
Presence*) that can be accomplished by his sons
and daughters in and through the flame of the
individual Christ Self. Jesus holds the office in
hierarchy of *World Teacher*. His *retreat* is the
Resurrection Temple, located in the *etheric*
realm over the Holy Land. He also serves in the
Arabian Retreat in the Arabian Desert north-
east of the Red Sea.

Karma. Sanskrit for action or deed. Karma is (1)
energy in action; (2) the law of cause and effect
and retribution. "Whatsoever a man soweth,
that shall he also reap" (Gal. 6:7). Thus the law
of karma decrees that from lifetime to lifetime
man determines his fate by his actions, including his thoughts, feelings, words, and deeds.

Karmic Board. *See* Lords of Karma.

Keepers of the Flame Fraternity. Founded in 1961
by *Saint Germain,* an organization of *chelas* of
the *ascended masters* who support the activities
of the *Great White Brotherhood* and the
dissemination of their teachings on earth and
who receive graded lessons in *cosmic law*
dictated by the ascended masters through their
messengers Mark and Elizabeth Prophet.

Kwan Yin. The ascended lady master. Known as
the Goddess of Mercy, she keeps the flame of
the *Divine Mother* on behalf of the people of
China, Asia, and the world. As the representative of the seventh *ray* on the *Karmic Board,*
she radiates the qualities of mercy, forgiveness,

and compassion to the evolutions of earth from her *etheric* temple over Peking, China. Kwan Yin has taken the vow of the bodhisattva to serve the planet earth until all her evolutions are free.

Lemuria. Mu, the lost continent of the Pacific which, according to the findings of James Churchward, archaeologist and author of *The Lost Continent of Mu,* extended from north of Hawaii three thousand miles south to Easter Island and the Fijis and was made up of three areas of land stretching more than five thousand miles from east to west. He estimates that Mu was destroyed approximately twelve thousand years ago by the collapse of the gas chambers which upheld the continent (*The Lost Continent of Mu* [New York: Ives Washburn, 1931], pp. 252, 282-83).

Light. Spiritual light is the energy of God, the potential of the *Christ.* As the essence of *Spirit,* the term "light" can be used synonymously with the terms "God," "Christ," and *"sacred fire."* It is the emanation of the *Great Central Sun* and the individualized *I AM Presence.*

Lord Maitreya. The *ascended master.* Together with Gautama, Maitreya followed the disciplines of the *Buddha* under *Sanat Kumara.* He holds the office of Cosmic *Christ* and Planetary Buddha, serving directly under Lord Gautama and directly over the *World Teachers.* He teaches mankind the *cosmic consciousness* of the Christ, its universality throughout *cosmos.* He is known as the Great Initiator and was, in fact, the initiator of *Jesus* in his personification of the individual *Christ Self* as an example to mankind. Lord Maitreya is the friend of all initiates of the *sacred fire*. When called upon, he will give the illumination of the Christ to pass the initiations which come through his hand.

Lords of Karma. The *ascended beings* who comprise the Karmic Board: The *Goddess of Liberty;* the *Great Divine Director; Portia,* the Goddess of Justice; the ascended lady master Nada; Pallas Athena, Goddess of Truth; *Kwan Yin,* Goddess of Mercy; and *Cyclopea.* These seven *ascended masters* dispense justice to this system of worlds. All *souls* must pass before the Karmic Board before and after each incarnation on earth. The Karmic Board, acting in consonance with the individual *I AM Presence* and *Christ Self,* determines when the soul has earned the right to be free from the wheel of *karma* and the round of rebirth.

Lucifer. From the Latin, meaning "light-bearer." One who attained to the rank of *archangel* and fell from grace through ambition, the pride of the ego, and disobedience to the laws of God. The *angels* who followed him are the fallen ones, also called Luciferians or sons of Belial, who have embodied among the children of God. (See the parable of the tares among the wheat, Matt. 13:24-30, 36-43.) Lucifer was bound by Michael the Archangel on April 16, 1975 and taken to the Court of the Sacred Fire on Sirius where he stood trial before the Four and Twenty Elders in the final judgment. He went through the second death on April 26, 1975. Many who followed the Fallen One in the Great Rebellion have also been brought to trial. *See also* Satan.

Luciferian. *See* Lucifer.

Macrocosm. From the Greek, meaning "great world." The larger *cosmos;* the entire warp and woof of creation which we call the *Cosmic Egg.* Also used to contrast man the *microcosm,* "the little world," against the backdrop of the larger world in which he lives. *See also* Microcosm.

Maha Chohan. The representative of the *Holy Spirit* to a planet and its evolutions. The *ascended master* who currently holds the office of Great Lord (Maha Chohan) over the seven lords (chohans) of the *rays* was embodied as the poet Homer. In his final embodiment in India, the *light* which he drew forth was a comfort to millions. The Maha Chohan maintains an *etheric* retreat with a physical focus on the island of Ceylon where the flame of the Holy Spirit is anchored. *See also* Chohan.

Manu. Sanskrit for the progenitor and lawgiver of the human race. The Manu and his divine complement are ascended *twin flames* assigned by the Father-Mother God to ensoul the archetypal pattern of the *Christ* for certain evolutions or lifewaves which comprise what is known as a *root race.*

Mass consciousness. The collective consciousness of humanity.

Mater. Latin for "mother." Mater is the *materialization* of the God flame, the feminine polarity of the Godhead. The term is used interchangeably with "Matter" to describe the planes of being that conform with the aspect of God as *Mother.* The *soul* that descends from the plane of *Spirit* abides in time and space in Mater for the purpose of its evolution that necessitates the mastery of time and space and of the energies of God through the correct exercise of *free will*. The four lower *bodies of man*, of a planet, and of systems of worlds occupy and make up the frequencies of Matter. *See also* Spirit.

Matter. *See* Mater.

Mental body. One of the four lower *bodies of man*; the body that is intended to be the vehicle for the mind of God or the *Christ* mind. "Let this mind be in you which was also in Christ *Jesus*" (Phil. 2:5). Until quickened, this body, often called the lower mental body, remains the vehicle for the *carnal mind*.

Messenger. One appointed by the *hierarchy* to deliver to mankind the dictations of the *ascended masters ex cathedra* in the power of the *spoken Word*. One who is trained by an ascended master to receive by various methods the words, concepts, teachings, and messages of the *Great White Brotherhood*. One who delivers the law, the prophecies, and the dispensations of God for a people and an age.

Microcosm. From the Greek meaning "small world." (1) The world of the individual, his *four lower bodies*, his *aura*, and the forcefield of his *karma*. (2) The planet. *See also* Macrocosm.

Misqualification (of energy). The "mist" qualification of fallen man and woman; the spawning of *evil*, or the energy *veil*, through the misuse of *free will* by the evolutions of time and space. The misapplication of God's energy. The use of God's energy to increase hatred instead of love; fear, doubt, and death instead of self-mastery; darkness instead of *light*, etc.

Misqualified energies. *See* Misqualification (of energy).

Monad. *See* Human monad.

Mother. "Mother," "Divine Mother," "World Mother," "universal Mother," and "Mother of the World" are alternate terms for the feminine polarity of the Godhead, the manifestation of God as Mother. Matter is the feminine polarity of *Spirit,* and the term is used interchangeably with *Mater,* Latin meaning "mother." In this context, the entire material *cosmos* becomes the womb of creation into which Spirit projects the energies of life. Matter, then, is the womb of the *Cosmic Virgin,* who also exists in Spirit as the spiritual polarity of God.

We recognize *Alpha and Omega* as the highest representatives of the Father-Mother God and often refer to Omega as the Divine Mother. Those who assume the feminine polarity of consciousness after the *ascension* are known as ascended lady masters. Together with all feminine beings in the ascended octaves, they focus the flame of the Divine Mother on behalf of the evolutions of mankind evolving in many systems of worlds. *See also* Mother of the Flame.

Mother Mary. The mother of *Jesus,* who ascended at the close of her Galilean embodiment. Her name means mother *ray (Ma ray).* She was embodied on *Atlantis* as a temple virgin and tended the flame in the Temple of Truth while learning the science of the immaculate concept which enabled her to give birth to the *Christ* in her final incarnation.

Mother of the Flame. An office of *hierarchy* held

successively by those unascended feminine
devotees appointed by the *Great White
Brotherhood* to nourish, or mother, the flame of
life in all mankind. In 1961 Clara Louise
Kieninger was named the first Mother of the
Flame of the *Keepers of the Flame Fraternity*
by *Saint Germain*. On April 9, 1966, that office
was transferred to Elizabeth Clare Prophet. At
that time Clara Louise Kieninger became the
Regent Mother of the Flame, an office which
she continues to hold from the ascended level.
See also Mother.

Mystery schools. Since the expulsion of man and
woman from the Garden of Eden (symbolizing
the pure consciousness of God) because of the
misuse of the *sacred fire* in the incorrect
application of *free will,* the *Great White
Brotherhood* has maintained mystery schools,
or *retreats* at the physical and *etheric plane*
which serve as a repository for the knowledge of
the sacred fire which is vouchsafed to man and
woman once they have demonstrated the
discipline necessary to keep the way of the *Tree
of Life*. The Essene Community was a mystery
school, as was the school at Crotona conducted
by Pythagoras. Other mystery schools were
located in India and Tibet for thousands of
years until they were destroyed by the forces of
darkness. Wherever these schools have been
destroyed, the masters who conducted them
have withdrawn to their retreats in the etheric
plane. Here they train their disciples between
embodiments and during sleep; here their *souls*
journey to attain that knowledge which until
this century has not been available to mankind
en masse in the physical plane.

Omega. *See* Alpha and Omega.

Pearls of Wisdom. Weekly letters of instruction dictated by the *ascended masters* to their *chelas* throughout the world through the *messengers* Mark and Elizabeth Prophet. The *Pearls of Wisdom* have been published by *The Summit Lighthouse* since 1958.

Physical body. The most dense of the four lower *bodies of man,* corresponding with the plane of earth; the body that is the vehicle for God's power and the focal point for the crystallization in form of the energies of the *etheric, mental,* and *emotional bodies.*

Portia. The ascended lady master. Goddess of Justice, representing the sixth *ray* of service and ministration on the *Karmic Board.* Also known as the Goddess of Opportunity, Portia holds the flame of justice and opportunity on behalf of the evolutions of earth. Portia and her *twin flame, Saint Germain,* are the directors of the next two-thousand-year cycle, the seventh dispensation known as the Aquarian age.

Power, wisdom, and love. The trinity of the *threefold flame*—power representing the Father, wisdom the Son, and love the *Holy Spirit.* The balanced manifestation of these God-qualities in and as the flame within the heart is the definition of Christhood.

Presence. *See* I AM Presence.

Psychic. From the word "psyche," meaning *soul.* The term "psychic" has come to be used synonymously with the term *"astral"* in its negative context and pertains to the penetration and manipulation of energy at the level of the *astral plane,* the probing of dimensions in time and space beyond the physical. According to the *ascended masters,* one who has involved his energies in what is known as the psychic, psychicism, or psychic phenomena is functioning on the lower astral plane and hence forgoes the opportunity to develop his ability to penetrate and manipulate the energies and octaves of *Spirit,* or God.

Rays. Beams of *light* or other radiant energy. The light emanations of the Godhead which, when invoked in the name of God or in the name of the *Christ,* burst forth as a flame in the world of the individual. Rays may be projected through the *God consciousness* of *ascended* or *unascended beings* as a concentration of energy taking on numerous God-qualities, such as love, truth, wisdom, healing, etc. Through the misuse of God's energy, certain unascended beings may project rays having negative qualities, such as death rays, sleep rays, hypnotic rays, disease rays, etc. *See also* Color rays.

Real Image. (1) The true image of God after which man (male and female) was made in the beginning (Gen. 1:26-27). The Real Image is the likeness of God; it is the blueprint of the true identity of the *sons and daughters of God.* (2) The face of God.

Real Self. The *Christ Self;* the *I AM Presence;* immortal *Spirit* that is the animating principle of all manifestation. *See also* Chart of Your Divine Self.

Retreats. Focuses of the *Great White Brotherhood* chiefly on the *etheric plane* where the *ascended masters* preside, anchoring one or more flames of the Godhead and the momentum of their service and attainment for the balance of *light* in the *four lower bodies* of a planet and its evolutions. Retreats serve many functions for the *hierarchy* administering to the lifewaves of Terra. Some retreats are open to unascended mankind, whose *souls* may journey there in the *etheric body* both between and during their incarnations on earth. The focus of the ascended masters *El Morya* and *Saint Germain* in Colorado Springs was consecrated as a physical retreat of the ascended masters on April 11, 1971, by *Omega,* who named it the Retreat of the Resurrection Spiral. Many of the masters' retreats were anchored in the physical during earth's earlier golden ages. After the Fall, the masters withdrew their flames and their focuses to the etheric plane, hence the term "retreat." For the opening of the retreats of the *chohans* of the *rays* following the *ascension* of Lanello, see *Pearls of Wisdom,* 11 March - 13 May 1973.

Root race. A group of *souls,* or a lifewave, who embody as a group and have a unique archetypal pattern, *divine plan,* and mission to fulfill on earth. According to esoteric tradition, there are seven primary aggregations of souls, i.e., the first to the *seventh root races.*

Sacred fire. God, *light,* life, energy, the I AM THAT I AM. "Our God is a consuming fire" (Heb. 12:29). The sacred fire is the precipitation of the Holy Ghost for the baptism of *souls,* for purification, for alchemy and transmutation, and for the realization of the sacred ritual of the return to the One.

Saint Germain. The *ascended master*. Lord *(Cho-han)* of the Seventh *Ray*. Hierarch of the Aquarian age, patron of the United States of America. Saint Germain was accorded the title "God of Freedom" because of his intense devotion to the flame of freedom and his attainment of the *cosmic consciousness* of that flame. He was embodied as Francis Bacon; Christopher Columbus; Merlin; Joseph, the protector of *Jesus* and Mary; and the prophet Samuel.

Sanat Kumara. The *ascended master*. Hierarch of Venus; one of the seven holy Kumaras who came to earth aeons ago to keep the *threefold flame* of life on behalf of mankind after their expulsion from Eden. Sanat Kumara established his *retreat* at Shamballa, an island in the Gobi Sea, now the Gobi Desert. The first to respond to his flame was Gautama *Buddha,* then *Lord Maitreya*. Sanat Kumara held the position of Lord of the World until his disciple Gautama Buddha reached sufficient attainment to hold that office. On January 1, 1956, Gautama Buddha was crowned Lord of the World and Sanat Kumara returned to Venus and to his *twin flame,* the lady master Venus.

Satan. A lieutenant of *Lucifer* and ranking member of the false *hierarchy*. The personification of *evil,* or the energy *veil*. The one who has deified evil and is therefore called the devil. Both Lucifer and Satan and their various lieutenants have been referred to as the adversary, the accuser of the brethren, the tempter, the Antichrist, the personification of the *carnal mind* of mankind, the serpent, the beast, the dragon, etc. *See also* Lucifer.

Serapis Bey. The *ascended master*. Lord *(Chohan)* of the Fourth *Ray;* Hierarch of the Ascension Temple at Luxor, Egypt; keeper of the *ascension* flame. Known as the great disciplinarian, Serapis reviews and trains candidates for the ascension.

Seven rays. *See* Color rays.

Seventh root race. An evolution of *souls* destined to embody on the continent of South America under the seventh dispensation, the Aquarian age, and the seventh *ray. See also* Root race.

Sin. Any departure from *cosmic law* that is the result of the exercise of *free will.*

Sons and daughters of God. (1) Those who come forth as the fruit of the divine union of the spirals of *Alpha and Omega;* those who have the potential to become the *Christ.* The creation of the Father-Mother God, made in the image and likeness of the Divine Us, identified by the *threefold flame* of life anchored within the heart. (2) On the Path the term "sons and daughters of God" denotes a level of initiation and a rank in *hierarchy* that is above those who are called the children of God—children in the sense that they have not passed the initiations of the *sacred fire* that would warrant their being called sons and daughters of God.

Soul. God is a Spirit and the soul is the living potential of God. The soul's demand for *free will* and its separation from God resulted in the descent of this potential into the lowly estate of the flesh. Sown in dishonor, the soul is destined to be raised in honor to the fullness of that God-estate which is the one Spirit of all Life. The soul can be lost; Spirit can never die.

The soul remains a fallen potential that must be imbued with the reality of Spirit, purified through prayer and supplication, and returned to the glory from which it descended and to the unity of the Whole. This rejoining of soul to Spirit is the alchemical marriage which determines the destiny of the self and makes it one with immortal Truth. When this ritual is fulfilled, the highest Self is enthroned as the Lord of Life and the potential of God, realized in man, is found to be the All-in-all. (See pp. 5-10 of *Climb the Highest Mountain* by Mark and Elizabeth Prophet.)

Spirit. The masculine polarity of the Godhead; the co-ordinate of *Matter;* God as Father, who of necessity includes within the polarity of himself God as *Mother* and hence is known as the Father-Mother God. The plane of the *I AM Presence,* of perfection; the dwelling place of the *ascended masters* in the Most High God. (When lower-cased, as in "spirits," the term is synonymous with discarnates, or disembodied *souls.)*

Spoken Word. The *Word* of the Lord God released in the fiats of the creation. The release of the energies of the Word, or the Logos, through the throat *chakra.* It is written, "By thy words thou shalt be justified, and by thy words thou shalt be condemned" (Matt. 12:37). When man and woman consecrate the throat chakra to the release of the Word of God, their word becomes a command that fulfills the law of creation.

Invocations given by priests and priestesses of the *sacred fire* on *Lemuria* in this power of the spoken Word were according to the science of the Logos. This science was used by the Israelites to fell the walls of Jericho. Today disciples use the power of the word in *decrees,* affirmations, and mantras to draw the essence of the sacred fire from the *I AM Presence,* from the *ascended masters,* the *Christ Self,* and *cosmic beings* and to channel these energies into matrices of transmutation and transformation in the planes of *Matter.* The alchemy of change is wrought by the power of the spoken Word. The master of the Aquarian age, *Saint Germain,* teaches his disciples to invoke, by the power of the spoken Word, the *violet flame* for forgiveness of sins and the baptism of the sacred fire in preparation for transition into the higher consciousness of God.

The Summit Lighthouse. An outer organization of the *Great White Brotherhood* founded by Mark L. Prophet in 1958 in Washington, D.C., under the direction of the ascended master *El Morya,* Chief of the *Darjeeling Council,* for the purpose of publishing and disseminating the teachings of the *ascended masters.*

Synthetic image. That aspect of man or woman which is the counterfeit of true selfhood. The synthetic image is diametrically opposed to the *Real Image* of the *Christ Self,* which is the true identity of the *sons and daughters of God.*

Threefold flame. The flame of the *Christ* that is the spark of life anchored in the heart *chakra,* or heart center, of the *sons and daughters of God* and the children of God. The sacred trinity of *power, wisdom, and love* that is the manifestation of the *sacred fire.*

Transfiguration. An initiation on the path of the *ascension* which takes place when the initiate has attained a certain balance and expansion of the *threefold flame.* (See Matt. 17:1-8.)

Tree of Life. "Out of the ground made the Lord God to grow every tree that is pleasant to the sight and good for food; the Tree of Life also in the midst of the garden, and the tree of knowledge of good and *evil*" (Gen. 2:9). The Tree of Life is symbolical of the *I AM Presence* of each individual. It is also referred to in the Book of Revelation: "In the midst of the street of it and on either side of the river was there the Tree of Life, which bare twelve manner of fruits and yielded her fruit every month: and the leaves of the tree were for the healing of the nations" (Rev. 22:2). The twelve manner of fruits thereof are the twelve qualities of the *God consciousness* which man and woman are intended to realize as they follow the initiations on the path of the *ascension*. These are God-power, God-love, and God-mastery; God-control, God-obedience, and God-wisdom; God-harmony, God-gratitude, and God-justice; God-reality, God-vision, and God-victory. (See chap. 3 of *Intermediate Studies of the Human Aura* by Djwal Kul, published by The Summit Lighthouse.)

Tube of light. The white *light* that descends from the heart of the *I AM Presence* in answer to the call of man as a shield of protection for his *four lower bodies* and his *soul* evolution. *See also* Chart of Your Divine Self.

Twin flame. The *soul's* masculine or feminine counterpart conceived out of the same white-fire core, the fiery ovoid of the *I AM Presence.*

Victory. The *ascended master.* A Venusian master whose devotion to the flame of victory for more than a hundred thousand years has given him the authority over that flame through vast reaches of the *cosmos*. Mighty Victory was one of the *cosmic beings* who responded to *Saint Germain's* call for cosmic assistance to the earth in the 1930s. He has twelve cosmic masters serving with him in addition to legions of *angels* and *ascended beings* who focus the consciousness of victory and the victorious sense to every *soul* evolving in the planes of *Matter*.

Violet flame. Seventh-*ray* aspect of the *Holy Spirit*. The *sacred fire* that transmutes the cause, effect, record, and memory of *sin*, or negative *karma*. Also called the flame of transmutation, of freedom, and of forgiveness. (See pp. 295-98 of *Climb the Highest Mountain* by Mark and Elizabeth Prophet, published by The Summit Lighthouse.) *See also* Chart of Your Divine Self.

Word. The Word is the Logos; it is the power of God and the realization of that power in the *Christ*. The energies of the Word are released by devotees of the Logos in the ritual of the science of the *spoken Word*. It is through the Word that the Father-Mother God communicates with mankind. The Christ is the personification of the Word. (See *The Science of the Spoken Word* by Mark and Elizabeth Prophet, published by The Summit Lighthouse.)

World Teacher. Office in *hierarchy* held by those *ascended beings* whose attainment qualifies them to represent the universal and personal *Christ* to unascended mankind. The masters *Jesus* and Kuthumi, who currently hold the office, are responsible for setting forth the teachings in this two-thousand-year cycle leading to individual self-mastery in the *Christ consciousness*.

Index

Aaron, challenged by the magicians, 36

Abandonment, a sense of, 34

Abraham, "...was called the Friend of God," 9

Abundance: a living, 25; manifest in nature, 64. *See also* Abundant life; Abundant living

Abundant life, the concept of the, 11. *See also* Abundance

Abundant living, 44; all deterrents to, knocked down, 67. *See also* Abundance

Accomplishments, calling attention to one's, 49

Action: invocation as invoked, 37; those successful in producing wrong, 35. *See also* Works

Addendum, continual, 33. *See also* Change

Adept(s): defined, 117; a mortal, 31; a true spiritual, 36; a wondrous secret held by, 38; the young, 39. *See also* Masters

Adhemar, Mme. d', 104

Advanced Studies in Alchemy, 84

Advancement of Learning, 100

Aesop, Lanello as, 111

Afflatus, the divine, 30

Age(s): degradations of past, 83; a new, born of the Spirit, 25. *See also* Aquarian Age; Golden age

Akashic records: defined, 117; entering into, 13

Akbar the Great, El Morya as, 134

Alban, St., Saint Germain as, 93-94

Alchemical arts, those successful in the, 37. *See also* Alchemy

Alchemical control, over emotions, 53. *See also* Alchemy

Alchemical creation, 62. *See also* Alchemy

Alchemical experiment(s), 37, 84. *See also* Alchemy

Alchemical expertise, a key by which, is developed, 81. *See also* Alchemy

Alchemical factors: great and vital, 34; the most important of all, 69. *See also* Alchemy

Alchemical feat(s), 9; that reflect selflessness, 36. *See also* Alchemy

Alchemical manifestation: the highest, 58; purity which precedes the greatest, 31; the sensitive matrices of, 69; visualization produces the, 48. *See also* Alchemy

Alchemical norm, the tether of the, 43. *See also* Alchemy

Alchemical precipitation, 37. *See also* Alchemy

Alchemical secrets, 70. *See also* Alchemy

Alchemical techniques, those who have irresponsibly used, 47. *See also* Alchemy

American Revolution, 105;
Saint Germain played a
role in the, 103
Amphibalus, 93
Anemic, spiritually, 17
Angel(s): angel devas, 133;
defined, 117; the language
of the, 24; let men entertain
you as, unawares, 50; the
tongues of, 21. *See also*
Angelic beings; Archangel;
Archeia; Fallen angels
Angelic beings, 71. *See also*
Angel(s)
Anna, 91
Anxieties: must go, 67; the
shedding of, 65. *See also*
Anxiety
Anxiety: most negative mani-
festations stem from, 61;
Saint Germain on, 61-62, 66;
stems from a lack of faith,
64; understanding that will
heal, 65. *See also* Anxieties
Apophthegms, 102
Appearance, if you wish a
more youthful, 48. *See also*
Countenance
Appearance world, illusions
of the, 33
Appreciation, new levels of
spiritual, 24
Apprehensions, unbalance
thinking, emotions, and the
entire psyche, 62
Aquarian Age: Ascended
Master of the, 105; the hier-
arch of the, 5. *See also*
Age(s)
Aquinas, Thomas, 114
Archangel, defined, 118. *See
also* Angel(s)
Archeia, defined, 119. *See
also* Angel(s)
Archetypes, 84
Ark: of the covenant, 89-90; a
voice from the, 91
Art: destructive trends in, 77;
works of, 54

Arthur, 94-95; the King, 113
Ascended master(s), 43; de-
fined, 119; the forte of the,
9; invoke the presence of
the, to assist you, 42; offer
energies for the good of
humanity, 60. *See also*
Brotherhood; Great White
Brotherhood; Hierarchy;
Immortals; Masters
Ascension: defined, 120; of
Saint Germain, 71, 102;
should you not win your, 51
Ascension Temple, at Luxor,
151
"Ashram Notes," 115
Astral body, 135; of earth, 53.
See also Emotional body;
Four lower bodies
Astral effluvia, the moon re-
flects, 54. *See also* Astral
energies
Astral energies, 83. *See also*
Astral effluvia; Astral
plane; Psychic
Astral plane, defined, 120. *See
also* Astral energies
Atlantis, 102, 137; explained,
120; Lanello was a priest of
the sacred fire on, 111;
Mother Mary embodied on,
145
Aton, God of the Sun, 111
Attachments, let men empty
themselves of, 72
Attainment, there are many
levels of, 48
Attitude(s): the correct sci-
entific, 14; incorrect, 15; a
proper, 44
Aura, defined, 121
Avatar, defined, 121
Awareness: a new sense of,
46; states of inner, 73

Bach, Johann Sebastian, the
classical music of, 23
Bacon, Francis, Saint Germain as, 99-102

body is under the, of the
Christ, 53. *See also* Control;
Power

Doomsday, anticipating a, 62

Door: each one must open
the, for himself, 74; the
golden, 80

Doubt(s), 11, 29; faith and,
29-30; and negation destroy,
75; projections of, 30; a
sense of, 34

Dove(s): "Be wise as ser-
pents and harmless as
doves!" 58; from heaven
perched upon Joseph's rod,
92

Drudgery, relieving mankind
of, 77

Drugs: dangerous, 35; the
taking of, 23

Duality, of life, 67

Earth: the astral body of, 53;
the bond between, and
heaven shall raise this star,
25; is one's own footstool
kingdom, 56; it is here on,
that we are obliged to create, 40; living according to
the "earth, earthy," 72;
man has been confined to
the, 70. *See also* Planet;
World

Ector, Sir, 94

Eden: access to, 72; the garden of, 27, 35, 48, 146; the
secrets of life contained in,
70; sword at the east of, 72

Edenic school, shall be reestablished, 48. *See also*
Eden

Effort(s): cosmic, 26; enormous, to assist humanity,
31; more advanced, 79; unrewarded, 15

Egg, cosmic, defined, 131-32

Ego(s), 14; divine, defined,
133; ego-expression, 22;
human, 31, 139; mystery

schools where the, is ca-
tered to, 63; a puppet to the
will of other, 39; rebellious,
78. *See also* Personality;
Self

Egypt, 92; the Saviour of, 93

El Morya, 134; offers energies for the good of humanity, 60; Mark L. Prophet
contacted by, 114; under-
took the training of the
messengers, 105

Electron(s): can become a
universe, 75; belief in the
power that keeps, in mo-
tion, 35

Elements in Physics, 94

Elements in Theology, 94

Elizabeth, Queen, 100

Emotional body: defined, 134-
35; the moon governs, 53.
See also Astral body; Emotions; Four lower bodies

Emotional control, 58. *See
also* Emotions

Emotional patterns, destructive, 21. See also Emotions

Emotions: alchemical con-
trol over, 53; apprehensions
unbalance, 62; the control
of the, 56; the dregs of turbulent, 69; directing, to do
exactly what you want, 55;
human, 57; when your, be-
come disturbed, 54. *See also*
Emotional body; Emotional
control; Emotional pat-
terns; Feeling; Feeling
world

Energies: composing one's
identity pattern, 57; controlled, 78; of creation are
dispensed each moment, 7;
destructive, which poured
through the Beatles, 23; dominion over one's, 58; misqualified, 14, 54, 63, 66; a
moment to wrest control of
your, 54. *See also* Energy

See also Man

Mendelssohn, Felix, the classical music of, 23-24

Mental body, defined, 144. See also Four lower bodies; Mind

Mephistopheles, Faust sold his soul to, 29

Merchant of Venice, The, 102

Mercy, "His mercy endureth for ever," 9

Merlin, Saint Germain as, 94-95

Messenger(s): defined, 144; El Morya undertook the training of the, 105

Metals: base, that make up the synthetic image, 44; the changing of base, into gold, 71

Michael, Archangel, 42, 119

Microcosm, defined, 144

Mighty, he who puts down the, from their seats, 79

Mind: carefully prepared, 73; the child, is the greatest, 69; childlike, 69; contact with the Higher, 38; the Divine, 36; entering into the childlike, 72; has the power to expand its circle of influence, 41; the Higher, 27; a sharpening of the, 46; that created man, 16. See also Carnal mind; Christ mind; Mental body; Mind of God

Mind of God: alchemist attunes with the, 50; infinite potential of the cosmic, 47; the innocent, 72; union with the, 17. See also Christ mind; Mind

Miracle(s), 36; magicians who produce seeming, 82; recorded in the gospels, 43; of saving grace, 64; that affect others, 49

Misqualification(s): of energy, 144; light covered with men's, 74; the trends toward, 22

Mistakes, when men learn to forgive and forget their, 10. See also Error(s)

Modred, 95, 113

Momentums: amplifying negative, 63; of destructivity, 70; that draw negative conditions of the outside world, 66

Monad, human, defined, 139

Money changers, 10

Montessori International, 105

Mood energies, 34

Moon: the cycle of the full, 54; Saint Germain on the, 53-54

Moore, Thomas, El Morya as, 134

Moralities, new, 21. See also Morality

Morality, increasing lack of, 22. See also Moralities

More, Sir Thomas, El Morya as, 134

Morgana La Fey, 113

Mortality: the laws of, 70; the token sacrifice of, 58

Mother: defined, 145; the Divine, 43; the frustrated, 55

Mother of the Flame, defined, 145-46

Mountain(s): the faith that moves, 73; "going up into the mountain," 46-47; holy, 59; to move, for the sake of greed, 31. See also Mountaintop experience; Summit

Mountaintop experience, 47. See also Mountain(s)

Mozart, Wolfgang Amadeus, the classical music of, 23

Mu, defined, 141

Muscle-bound, man is mentally, 17

Music: destructive trends in, 77; sacred, aborted through

astral and voodoo rhythms, 21; seek out classical, 23; those commissioned by the Brotherhood to bring forth the, of the spheres, 24. *See also* Jazz

Mystery: divine, 16; a penetrable, 86. *See also* Secret(s)

Mystery schools: defined, 146; where the ego is catered to, 63

Napoleon, 104

Nation(s): the contributing spirit of the, 58; the healing of the, 42

Nature: innocence of, 69; the pristine beauties of, 68; a stable God-intended control over, 65

Need(s): how to meet the, of our brethren, 64; open your heart to the, of the world, 43; what you have, of God will supply, 52

Negation, doubt and, destroy, 75. *See also* Negative conditions; Negative influences; Negatives; Nihilism

Negative conditions, momentums that draw, of the outside world, 66. *See also* Negation

Negative influences, eliminating, within and without one's world, 34. *See also* Negation

Negatives: amplifying our, instead of our positives, 63; counteracting all your, 51; people have nothing to lose but their, 72. *See also* Negation

New Atlantis, 101

Nexus, the recording, 8

Nihilism, Faust sold his soul to the forces of, 29. *See also* Negation

Ninny, the nebulous, 56

Nobility: creating, in the soul, 30; supreme, 9

Noblesse oblige, defined, chap. VIn.2

Noises, brutal, 21

Novum Organum, 101

Obedience, the Great Alchemist demands absolute, 21

Offspring, the blessing given by God at the birth of his, 56. *See also* Children

Oneness, with the Creator, 36. *See also* Union; Unity

Opportunity, lost, 8

Options, the spiritual, 26

Opus Majus, 96

Opus Minus, 96

Opus Tertium, 96

Order: infectious spirit of rebellion against, 35-36; templed, 76

Origen, Lanello as, of Alexandria, 112

Pain, understanding that will heal, 65

Pallas Athena, 101

Past, he who is willing to forsake a, 86. *See also* History

Patience, in your, possess ye your souls, 18

Pattern(s): creating according to the, made in the heavens, 12; creating after the, of the divine seed, 8; eternal, 18; in the heavens transform the patterns in the earth, 54; the necessary cosmic, 14; a perfect cosmic, 16. *See also* Design(s); Stereotypes

Paul, 38, 67, 112; the wondrous final change of which, spoke, 44

Peace, City of, 79

Peking, etheric temple over, 141

Projections, of doubt, 30

Promised Land, America as the, 101

Prophecy, that "One shall be taken, and the other left," 59

Prophet(s): "O Jerusalem, Jerusalem, thou that killest the prophets....," 70; Saint Germain as Samuel the, 89-91

Prophet, Mark L., 111-15; contacted by El Morya, 114

Proverb, the ancient, 22

Providence, the outworkings of, 24. *See also* God

Psalms, meditations recorded in the Book of, 55

Psyche, 62; forces imbedded in the, 63. *See also* Soul

Psychedelic perversions, 35

Psychic, defined, 147-48. *See also* Astral energies; Psychically inclined

Psychically inclined, those who have been, 43. *See also* Psychic

Puppet, to the will of other egos, 39

Purification, violet flame called forth for, 14. *See also* Catharsis; Cleansing

Purity, 73; the prism of, 54; which precedes the greatest alchemical manifestation, 31

Pythagoras, 112; the school at Crotona conducted by, 146

Qualification, where there is no, 8

Qualities: Christlike, 57; inherent God-qualities, 49; a purging of all undesirable, 63. *See also* Virtue(s)

Race, elder gods of the, 71

Radiance: a milky white, 40; of the Source, 49

Radioactive principle, of the expanding God consciousness, 11. *See also* Radioactive substance

Radioactive substance, 49. *See also* Radioactive principle

Rainbow rays, white contains all of the, 29. *See also* Rays

Rakoczy, founder of the House of, 137. *See also* Rakoczy Mansion

Rakoczy, Prince, Saint Germain as, 102-5

Rakoczy Mansion, 102. *See also* Rakoczy

Rays: the archangels and archeiai of the, 118-19; defined, 148. *See also* Color rays; Rainbow rays

Reactor, a cosmic, 59

Real: the cloud expands to contact all that is, 43; confidence in the, 67; a sense of the, 10. *See also* Reality

Reality: cultivation of the inner sense of, 73; man's realization of his God-reality, 82; power to sense shades of, 28; *summum bonum* of ultimate, 79; that which is tethered to, can never be lost, 72; the tides of, 23. *See also* Real

Realization, self-realization, 64, 78

Reason, the hallowed circle of, 16

Rebellion: the game to draw youth into, 21-22; the Great, 118; infectious spirit of, against order, 35-36; is as the sin of witchcraft, 90; the luciferian, 118

Recognition: be careful not to seek, for service, 49; striving only for outer, 85

Redeemer, the Divine, 74

Reembodiment. *See* Reincarnation

Summit University®

In every age there have been some, the few, who have pursued an understanding of God and of selfhood that transcends the current traditions of doctrine and dogma. Compelled by a faith that knows the freedom of love, they have sought to expand their awareness of God by probing and proving the infinite expressions of his law. Through the true science of religion, they have penetrated the 'mysteries' of both Spirit and Matter and come to experience God as the All-in-all.

Having discovered the key to reality, these sons and daughters of God have drawn about them disciples who would pursue the disciplines of the law of the universe and the inner teachings of the 'mystery schools'. Thus Jesus chose his apostles, Bodhidharma his monks, and Pythagoras his initiates at Crotona, Gautama Buddha called his disciples to form the *sangha* (community), and King Arthur summoned his knights to the quest for the Holy Grail at the Table Round.

Summit University is a mystery school for men and women of the twentieth century who would pursue the great synthesis of the teachings of the ascended masters—the few who have overcome in every age, the many who now stand as our elder brothers and sisters on the Path. Together Gautama Buddha and Lord Maitreya sponsor Summit University with the World Teachers Jesus and Kuthumi, El Morya, Lanello, and Saint Germain, Confucius, Mother Mary, Moses and Mohammed, the Archangels Michael and Gabriel, and "numberless numbers" of "saints robed in white"—the Great 'White' Brotherhood. To this university of the Spirit they lend their flame, their counsel, the momentum of their attainment, and the living teaching for us who would follow in their footsteps to the source of that reality they have become.

Founded in 1971 under the direction of the Messengers Mark L. Prophet and Elizabeth Clare Prophet, Summit University currently holds three twelve-week retreats each year—fall, winter, and spring quarters—as well as summer sessions. All of the courses are based on the unfoldment of the inner potential of the Christ, the Buddha, and the Mother. Through the teachings of the ascended masters given through their messengers, students at Summit University pursue the disciplines on the path of the ascension for the soul's ultimate reunion with the Spirit of the living God.

This includes the study of the sacred scriptures of East and West taught by Jesus and Gautama; exercises in the self-mastery of the energies of the chakras and the aura under

Kuthumi and Djwal Kul; beginning and intermediate studies in alchemy under the Ascended Master Saint Germain; the Cosmic Clock—a new-age astrology for charting the cycles of karma and dharma given by Mother Mary; the science of the spoken Word in conjunction with prayer, meditation, and visualization—the key to soul liberation in the Aquarian age; weekly healing services, "Be Thou Made Whole!" at the Ashram of the World Mother in which the messenger gives personal and planetary healing invocations; the psychology of the family, the marriage ritual and meditations for the conception of new-age children; counseling for community service through the sacred labor; the teachings and meditations of the Buddha taught by Gautama Buddha, Lord Maitreya, Lanello, and the five Dhyani Buddhas; and individual initiations transferred to each student from the ascended masters through the messengers.

Summit University is a twelve-week spiral that begins with you as self-awareness and ends with you as God Self-awareness. As you traverse the spiral, light intensifies, darkness is transmuted. You experience the rebirth day by day as the old man is put off and the new man is put on. Energies are aligned, chakras are cleared, and the soul is poised for the victorious fulfillment of the individual divine plan.

In addition to preparing the student to enter into the Guru/chela relationship with the ascended masters and the path of initiation outlined in their retreats, the academic standards of Summit University, with emphasis on the basic skills of both oral and written communication, prepare students to enroll in top-level undergraduate and graduate programs and to become efficient members of the national and international community. A high school diploma (or its equivalent) is required and a willingness to become the disciplined one—the disciple of the Great God Self of all.

Summit University is a way of life that is an integral part of Camelot—an Aquarian-age community secluded on a beautiful 218-acre campus in the Santa Monica Mountains west of Los Angeles near the beaches of Malibu. Here ancient truths become the law of everyday living to hundreds of kindred souls brought together again for the fulfillment of the mission of the Christ through the oneness of the Holy Spirit.

For information write or call Summit University, Box A, Malibu, CA 90265   (213) 880-5300.

Summit University ☯ Press®